Life's Lessons

Evolving Strong Democracy by Sharing Success

Ann Miller

Life's Lessons -
Evolving Strong Democracy by Sharing Success

Copyright © 2016 by Ann Miller

This book is dedicated to people everywhere who are willing to work together in partnership to heal and unite our divided world and to create a kinder and more peaceful future for everyone.

"Each of us literally chooses, by his way of attending to things, what sort of Universe he shall appear to himself to inhabit."
William James

"To cultivate kindness is a valuable part of the business of life."
Samuel Johnston

CONTENTS

Lesson Two: Revolution and Wealth Creation

1. The Industrial Revolution
2. The Age of Reason
3. The Wealth of Nations
4. All men are crated equal
5. The Scottish-American billionaire – Andrew Carnegie
6. The American billionaire – Henry Ford

Lesson Three: Public Welfare and Power Elites

1. The power of the collective
2. The power elite
3. Social networking and controlling vested interests
4. Public welfare and a life with dignity
5. A strong social conscience

PART FOUR: Where Do We Go From Here?

1. Rethinking our value system
2. The tipping point
3. Links between individuals and community
4. A Strong Social Conscience
5. Using Power Wisely
6. Ethics and Corruption
7. Foreign Policy
8. Compassion, Knowledge and Wisdom

CONCLUSION: Creating a Hopeful Future

1. Putting People First
2. Accepting the Responsibilities of Citizenship
3. Learning Life's Lessons
4. Living with Dignity
5. Reaching the Limit

THE CREATIVE LEARNING SERIES

INTRODUCTION

An Abridged Edition of Life's Lessons

Evolving Strong Democracy by Sharing Success

Evolving Strong Democracy by Sharing Success is a special Abridged Edition of *Life's Lessons* which is designed to be an introduction to the Democracy elements of *The Creative Learning Series,* and, in particular, Book Eight in the series, *Building Wiser Democracies – An International Active Citizen Project,* and Book Thirteen, *The Creative Lifelong Learning Formula – Building Global Partnerships for a Sustainable World.*

The reason for offering this Abridged Edition is that it gives you the key principles and techniques of the *Creative Learning* system, as it relates to advancing democracy, enabling you to progress to the whole *Creative Learning Series.* If you then decide to focus further on transforming Education, Business or Government, you can move on to the whole book, or you may decide that you want to explore other books in the series, and you will have a good grounding to enable you to move forward. There is no particular order to the rest of the series – you choose what appeals to you to continue your Creative Lifelong Learning.

The full version of *Life's Lessons - Working Together to Transform Education, Business and Government*, which is available as a book or an E-Book, examines in detail the three organisational principles of Education, Business and Government which involve all of us in one way or another. It examines their development throughout the world since 1776, and seeks to shed light on how we might refocus our values, and create a more inclusive society, by designing education systems which are more about people than performance, businesses which are more about people than profit and governments which are about more about people than politics.

This Abridged Edition also looks at the development of Democracy from 1776, and invites you to consider in your particular way how we might redesign our democracies to focus more on a New Democracy Trifecta of people, relationships and infrastructure.

1. People

Everyone counts as part of our Global Human Potential, and we progress by nurturing the potential of each person and by providing good healthcare, good education and good work. The individual in a democratic society expects to be respected as an equal, and to be rewarded for good work, creativity and innovation. Social Justice and Social Inclusion are strong aspects of wise democracies which value individuals and put the fundamental Human Rights of freedom from fear and want at their core.

2. Relationships

Our Socio-Economic relationships are what help us to maximize our Human Potential, and wise democracies ensure that strong social and economic relationships are forged between all sections of society. Harnessing human potential means valuing our individual and collective knowledge, training and experience, which provides an advantage for human progress. A balanced approach to job creation, spending and taxation creates a successful society where every person is included in the success.

3. Infrastructure

Wise democratic governments develop systems, policies and procedures which allow people to function optimally and flourish. The infrastructure of a democratic society includes a wise consideration of Environmental Sustainability, not only locally but also globally. The resources of our Earth are our precious common inheritance and wise stewardship is our joint responsibility. Within states, controlling partisanship is a necessity for this continuous work to be accomplished even with changing governments.

Why rethink the script?

The Capitalist Democracy model which has been pursued since 1945 has now run its course. Reconstructing post-war economies and fostering growth was seen as the priority after WWII, and international competition helped achieve that goal, spurring citizens on to greater effort. Consolidating Capitalist Democracy was also seen as a bulwark against Communist Dictatorship, which was seen as a carry-over from pre-1945 totalitarianism. The world today, seventy years on, is a vastly different place, and we need to find a new way to think about what we want our democracies to be, and how we will achieve that goal.

We have all evolved and our social, economic and environmental knowledge and understanding have evolved as well. To put what we have learned into practice requires that we change how we frame our idea of Democracy, and that is what this project invites you to do. Our intrinsic motivation to improve how we all live our lives is what we will harness here. Human behaviour is an individual and collective choice, and choosing wisely depends on thinking carefully about the options and alternatives, and setting meaningful goals.

The idea here is to explore how we can re-define and re-energize our democracies using the *New Democracy Trifecta of People, Relationships and Infrastructure* as the framework, to increase personal, socio-economic and environmental wellbeing to benefit everyone.

1. **People** – Personal wellbeing for every citizen.
2. **Relationships** – Socio-economic wellbeing for every society.
3. **Infrastructures** – Environmental wellbeing for the entire world.

Our success in this venture will result in the creation of a more hopeful future for everyone, and that seems a worthy aim for our Democracy, which started out so long ago to advance happiness in the world by sharing the success which was previously enjoyed by so few in every society.

PART ONE

Why Change?

Are you happy with the way things are in the world today? Do you think things need to change? Do you feel helpless and frustrated in the midst of all the solutions delivered by so-called experts? I want to examine our social contracts, the way we relate to one another, and see whether we can make a change which will result in a better world. If so, how would we start?

"Change your mind and you change your life," the adage says. There is nothing as important as your attitude—it is the main determinant of success, and a positive attitude is your most important asset. This is a book designed to change your focus, to change how you see things, and, by doing that, to change your world and mine. A paradigm shift is when we all decide to change our focus—here, we will examine how we might achieve that change, starting with the institutions of education, business and government.

Socrates said the unexamined life is not worth living, but it seems that the over-examined life is the one we are living now, and we're suffering from the paralysis of over-analysis:

- The financial markets are in disarray, and nobody is confident that the measures that have been adopted are going to get us out of the mess we're in.

- The environment is in a mess, but how will we sustain our life styles without continuing to extract the level of resources that we've become used to.

- We live under the threat of global terrorism, and religious tensions threaten to erupt with the fervour of a medieval crusade or inquisition.

- Our education systems are allegedly not delivering what we need to compete in the modern world.

- Our businesses are struggling to survive in the current financial situation and the competition of global markets is threatening jobs.

- Our governments are raising taxes, tightening belts, and treating energy as an economic policy rather than as a social programme.

I think we'd all agree that something needs to change to make the world a better place, but what can it be? Is there one answer, or is it far too complicated for one answer? I want to look at a new framework, a *Democracy Trifecta, of People, Relationships and Infrastructure*, to see if there is a way to design a simple strategy we can all use to make a difference to how our democracies work for the people in them.

Every event and experience in life is part of a universal curriculum—every situation is a lesson in growing into our full potential, as individuals and as the race which is human. This book is the second in the Creative Learning Series, and is designed to enable you to take a fresh look at how we think about our democracies. Your job is to decide what you can contribute to change your world and mine.

Three Scotsman have significantly influenced the direction of this work—Adam Smith, economist and philosopher, John MacMurray, philosopher, and Andrew Carnegie, philanthropist and billionaire. Each made a significant impact in his own field, as well as having a wider impact on other thinkers and doers, and each continues to make a difference to lives to this day. You, too, have a gift to bring to the world, and although your impact may not be as significant as the above three men, nevertheless, you can make a difference to how things are now, and to what they will become in the future.

What you do is more important than what you think, believe or say, but action starts with beliefs and thoughts. I encourage you to keep notes of the various thoughts which cross your mind as you read—a journal is a good place to do this, as, like a diary, it is something which you can refer to again and again and something which helps you to keep track of changing circumstances. Creativity is a human given—we are all creative because we are human, and we have the will and the power to change things. Above all, what I want you to do is *act to change what needs to be changed*, in whatever small way you can, and believe that it matters that you do.

1. Two Scottish Philosophers

One of my favourite philosophers is the Scotsman, John Macmurray (1891–1976), and some of his ideas have significantly influenced the direction and style of this work:

- Action is more important than knowledge, belief or faith.
- Authority should be our guide and not our master; tradition should be our starting point and not our resting place.
- We must experiment with our knowledge and beliefs with the express purpose of proving them valid or otherwise.
- Every civilisation has a pivotal idea which gives it purpose, direction and meaning.

John Macmurray's 1953–54 Gifford Lectures at Edinburgh University were published in two volumes—*Self as Agent (1957)* and *Persons in Relation (1961)*, and Tony Blair, British Prime Minister, acknowledged Macmurray's influence on him in his foreword to the Macmurray anthology published in 1996:

"I also find him immensely modern…in the sense that he confronted what will be the critical political question of the twenty-first century: the relationship between individual and society."

We are currently dealing with the effects of the clash of self-interest and social justice—individuals still seek to be rich; corporations still pursue wealth; governments still pursue power through production, financial influence and natural resources. Meanwhile we have great poverty and hardship at home and abroad. Unlimited economic growth is an illusion, and natural resources are finite, but we still persist in pursuing an agenda which needs to be revised, an agenda set during the Industrial Revolution of the eighteenth century.

In 1776, Adam Smith, Scottish Economist and Moral Philosopher, published *The Wealth of Nations*; the newly formed American congress published the *Declaration of Independence*; and Edward Gibbon published the first volume of the *Decline and Fall of the Roman Empire*. The juxtaposition of these three events is not without a certain irony, given current events.

The Wealth of Nations is considered to be the foundation of modern economic theory, and has continued to influence authors, economists, governments and business organisations since it was published. Its advocacy of free markets as more productive and beneficial to their societies is still the central dogma of the modern free trade argument.

"As every individual…neither intends to promote the public interest, nor knows how much he is promoting it…he intends only his own security…he intends only his own gain, and he is in this, as in many other cases, led by an invisible hand to promote an end which was no part of his intention. Nor is it always the worse for the society that it was no part of it. By pursuing his own interest he frequently promotes that of the society more effectually than when he really intends to promote it."
Adam Smith
The Wealth of Nations (1776)

2. Uncontrolled Greed or Checks and Balances

I think we are very clear that when people intend to pursue their own interests without concern for the effect on others, we end up precisely where we are now. The uncontrolled greed released by the economic policies of the past thirty years confirms the need for close scrutiny and regulation. Allowing the financial markets to "police themselves" has not worked for the good of all, and has certainly not promoted the needs of society as a whole. It has created wealth, but only for those who have learned how to exploit the markets for their own gain.

George Stigler, the American Economist who won the 1982 Nobel Prize, developed the Economic Theory of Regulation, also known as "*capture*", which states that interest groups and other political participants will use the regulatory and coercive powers of government to shape laws and regulations in a way that is most beneficial to them. When the powerful lobby that stands to gain most from maintaining the status quo also holds the keys to the kingdom of government, we do indeed have to be clear that we must all understand the rules of the game. He who sets the fox to guard the chicken coop stands to lose all of his chickens.

Adam Smith's *Wealth of Nations* is often cited as the foundation text for the benefits of freedom to trade, but, to be fair to Adam Smith, his work has been subject to very selective reading by staunch advocates of fair trade and de-regulation, who are careful not to draw attention to Adam's statements about taxing the rich, and government's role in controlling their excesses. He also warns government of its duty to protect ordinary working people:

"…labouring poor, that is, the great body of the people who will suffer unless government takes some pains to prevent it…The necessities of life occasion the great expense of the poor. They find it difficult to get food, and the greater part of their little revenue is spent getting it. The luxuries and vanities of life occasion the principal expense of the rich, and a magnificent house embellishes and sets off to the best advantage all the other luxuries and vanities which they possess. A tax on house rents, therefore, would in general fall heaviest on the rich…It is not very unreasonable that the rich should contribute to the public expense, not only in proportion to their revenue, but something more than in that proportion."

Adam Smith was a canny Scot, a modest man, who passionately wanted to make things better for the poor. He was born in Kirkcaldy, in Scotland (as I was), and his father died when he was young. His friends were all social reformers, living in Scotland in the period after the 1745 Stuart Rebellion, the aftermath of which was brutal and merciless.

The members of Adam Smith's intellectual circle were themselves leaders of a social revolution which is still with us, and all of them wanted working people to be self-determining. In the mid-eighteenth century, that could only mean being an artisan, and controlling your own destiny by making money. The people who had made a living from the land had been evicted, and many of them would make their way to America, the land of the free, where there was the chance of a fresh start, free land, and relief from persecution, religious and racial.

John Stuart Mill, related to the Stuart kings, writing sixty years after Adam Smith, also believed that economic democracy was necessary in the capitalist economy to end dictatorial management and establish liberty and equality, but recognised the meaning of "wealth" beyond the material, and argued that the logical conclusion of unlimited growth was the destruction of the environment and a subsequent reduced quality of life.

In *The Principles of Political Economy (1848),* he concluded that a stationary state or plateau was inevitable within a world with finite natural resources:

"I cannot, therefore, regard the stationary state of capital and wealth with the unaffected aversion so generally manifested towards it by political economists of the old school. If the earth must lose that great portion of its pleasantness which it owes to things that the unlimited increase of wealth and population would extirpate from it, for the mere purpose of enabling it to support a larger, but not a better or happier population, I sincerely hope, for the sake of posterity, that they will be content to be stationary, long before necessity compel them to it."

3. Re-Asserting True Values

The point I want to focus on here is that we have been seduced into thinking that wealth and the creation of wealth is somehow the be-all-and-end-all of existence. In this, we can lose our grasp of the meaning of true values. If we are not careful what we admire, we encourage behaviour which is not helpful or admirable. Without in any way being moralistic, we can look with some shame at the people the popular media holds up for our admiration, through the proliferation of celebrity programming.

We are assailed by images of "life-styles of the rich and famous", and people are encouraged to "be a celebrity" of some sort or another—we have reality television, where people bare all, sometimes literally, for a moment of fame. No distinction is made between people who make a difference in the world by helping others, and those who embarrass themselves in public. Fame seems to be valuable in itself, irrespective of behaviour. Certain movie and sports stars court fame, and gain valuable publicity, even while they appear in the court of law, on charges for one misdemeanour or another. Infidelity and scandal are the order of the day, and the only censure is a shaking of the head and a wry smile.

How we manage to recover from the global financial events of the past few years is only one part of the world-shaking changes we are facing, and will continue to face, in the not-too-distant future. Far from enjoying a world of peace and prosperity, we are still enmeshed in war and poverty. While Adam Smith advocated progressive taxation, and the disproportionate taxation of income, he also noted that if governments could borrow without check, they would be more likely to wage war without check, and would also be likely to impose the burden on future generations.

Yet all is not gloom and doom. We have many things to be proud of, and there is more goodwill in the world than bad. Our collective institutions have been developed over the years since World War Two particularly, based firmly on the principles of social justice. Our intentions are admirable, but they have to be backed up by concerted action based on sound principles. Idealism alone is merely self-delusion.

As John Macmurray observed, human nature is inherently social:

"There are few things that I desire to do…which do not depend upon the active cooperation of others…I need you in order to be myself."

Macmurray was also aware that there was a need for healing in society:

"Until we are healed we cannot act healthily…what we have to do is…to cease our fruitless attempt to save ourselves…"

4. Working Together For a Better Future

What John Macmurray is referring to here is the importance of working together, in relationship, to solve the problems of society, local and international. It's not a case of selfishly pursuing your own fortune, and letting the less fortunate take their chances. As long as poverty is amongst us, we will never be able to make progress to the next stage of our evolution. We will keep going round the same loop, and the people who are struggling or suffering will always have feelings of despair, which can roll over into lawlessness or violence.

I want to explore with you the history and evolution of our Collective Society through the writings of some of our most creative thinkers. The fertile suggestions for meaningful change which they proposed are just as valid today as they were when they were put forward. What has changed is the context. Perhaps our world is more ready to re-examine its assumptions than when we enjoyed the perceived endless abundance of the last century. We need to choose to do things differently—we need to think about creating a *healthy world* rather than just a *wealthy world*.

The culmination of the technological revolution which started in the Agricultural and Industrial Revolutions of the eighteenth and nineteenth centuries is upon us now. The values which were entirely valid at that time and in that context need to be reviewed in the light of changing circumstances, and the evolution of our knowledge and understanding. We have learned the necessary lessons to enable us to survive and find food, but now we need to move on to discover how we can all thrive. We have exploited the natural resources of the earth with our increasingly rapacious technologies for two hundred years—the earth is groaning under the strain, and we have unleashed a domino-effect within our ecological system, which threatens the delicate balance devised by nature over millennia.

If every dark cloud has a silver lining, now is the time when we must urgently address the paradigm on which we have built our civilisations. Despite our surface differences, our needs are surprisingly similar—we thrive by maintaining a balanced relationship between the human economy and the health of the environment. If we place monetary gain above the welfare of people and the wellbeing of the world, we do so at our peril. The Clash of Civilisations may be the least of our worries if we don't change our ways.

Ecology is the study of living organisms in relation to their physical and biological environment—the ecosystem is a complex web of relationships involving a living community and its non-living setting. We have inadvertently allowed our attention to be diverted from our ecologies by concentrating all of our intellectual energies on our economies—the delicate balance has been compromised.

"Our problem is the unsustainability of the world we have created, and we should be clear that we can't solve this problem with the same consciousness that gave rise to it… because consciousness in the social, political and cultural context is the sum total of our view of the world, with its values, aspirations and background assumptions. It's the "paradigm" that underlies the way we think and the way we set our priorities."
Erwin Laszlo

5. Choosing To Change

Yet the "advanced Nations" persist in the now moribund mindset which sees the only way forward as a Darwinian struggle for survival where we progress by:

- continuing the competition for growth between the economies of advanced nations
- using cooperation only as a means to an economic end
- pursuing an end point which is for current rich nations to remain rich

Instead of concentrating on re-establishing a balance in a fair world, where all states enjoy the benefits of our current technologies of resource extraction and production, we continue with a system derived from a colonial past, where the advanced nations of Europe grew by exploiting the resources of whole continents—Africa, Asia, Australia, America and Antarctica and their oceans.

The Global Crisis is not only about resource scarcity and economics—it is about the disharmony of the whole system, and our insistence on maintaining a system whose time is past. Our value system needs to acknowledge the changes of the last one hundred years—material, physical, intellectual and spiritual—and re-invent itself in the new image of Social Justice. Social Justice means that everybody gets a fair share and a fair chance to succeed.

Fair distribution of resources and wealth is the only way forward and that will require an "adjustment" by the nations who got there first. That adjustment will happen by force if we don't acknowledge the necessity for change. Wherever we put our attention will grow—man is a creative animal, and we have been more successful than any other, not only in using the Earth's resources, but also in plundering them. In some cases, we have fouled our planet home to a perilous degree.

Corporations pursue wealth; governments pursue power; nature will not be bent to the will of either. Creating harmony with nature requires cooperation and respect—peace amongst states, and respect for our common environment and the living systems upon which all civilisations depend. The economic markets can't guide humanity's destiny—they are there to serve our needs, not rule them. We have inadvertently given wealth the upper hand over the health of the world.

All is certainly not well, but it could be, and it will be, if our human genius is brought to bear with piercing focus on turning things round by keeping humans and our planet flourishing and healthy. We need to change something significant if we are to make a difference—we need to change our ways, and to do that we need to change our mindset.

That's what I want you to think about if you decide to take this course in Life's Lessons. There are only three lessons set out here, and each of them has advice from some of our wisest thinkers throughout time. We are very smart as a species, but we need to get wise, fast:

In learning lies knowledge, and in knowledge lies wisdom.

PART TWO

What Needs to Change?

We live in a world dominated by economics, and the vocabulary and ethics of economics likewise dominates all of our organisations. Economics is the study of the production, distribution and consumption of goods and services, and it has an important role in our survival, but it is not an ideology—it is a functional process for survival.

Now that we have evolved the means of production to produce food and goods, the outcome of the Agricultural and Industrial Revolutions, and have evolved intellectually and emotionally enough to understand the necessity of individual and social freedom, the outcome of Civil Rights Movements, we need to think again about the central idea which gives meaning to our lives. We need to think about how everybody in the world can enjoy social justice, not just the fortunate few—we achieve social justice by practising social solidarity, and clarifying our social contracts.

The word "economics" stems from a Greek word meaning "household management", and economics touches on many disciplines— mathematics, sociology, psychology, accounting, geography and political theory. The attempt to build economic models is notoriously difficult because predictions of human behaviour en masse have proved unreliable, and many economists regard their subject as more of an art than a science.

Despite this, all of our organisations have adopted management systems based on the methods and values of the so-called "science of economics". We've inadvertently taken the "human" out of the equation, so that even our schools and hospitals are described as cost centres which must make a profit.

The idea that "the only valid success is tied to wealth" results in the validation of "fierce competition", "winning at any human cost" and the ultimate importance of "the bottom line". We turn human values into numbers, and caring services into accountability machines. We've made individualism more important than individuality, and promoted individualism over relationship.

Furthermore, we have created a whole industry dedicated to teaching people how to win by the pursuit of profit. The first step in this is to learn the vocabulary, grammar and syntax of financial success, so we have the proliferation of "management trainers", teaching business jargon to would-be "industry leaders", who'll learn the psychology of "getting ahead", setting up their own companies to sell the message. Only those who are willing and able to learn the "business-speak" can play the game to win.

Yesterday's ghastly corporate gobbledygook is translated into new techno-babble, and repackaged in cyber-space to reach an even bigger world-wide audience. Marshall McLuhan, the Canadian communication theorist who coined the phrases "the medium is the message" and "global village", predicted how language and the media would increasingly both reflect and mould the cultural aspirations of people.

In a culture where advertising agencies, analysts and spin doctors package and present people and products for our consumption, all in the name of profit, we require, more than ever, to be astute judges of real and fabricated "need". I want you to be aware of this dimension as you read each of the ten "lessons" in this "course"—much of what we have come to accept as a "human given" is due to the unconscious effect of media perspectives, which we now receive subconsciously and subliminally from a multitude of sources. It is part of the "hidden curriculum" of our lives.

1. Words Have Power

Communication is central to social change and transformation, and our assumptions and aspirations are embodied in our choice of language. The words and structures that we use to communicate our intentions are not detachable instruments of thought—the subliminal messages embodied in these systems are powerful influences on our psychological and social states:

- Education becomes all about the bottom line and efficiency outcomes, profit centres and products—the quality of teaching and learning is judged by the outcomes of formal tests, notoriously biased in favour of candidates who can learn the skills necessary to pass tests. Adjusting to the demands of formal education is itself a skill-set, taught in our elite schools, and continued into the university system of Masters and PhDs, where one of the courses is how to write your paper so that it meets the demands of the system. All of this tends towards conformity with an existing paradigm. In today's world, Lifelong Learning is a necessity and finding ways to make learning accessible to everyone is the challenge.

- Business becomes about ruthless exploitation and profit above people. Rather than people having pride in being employed in a certain capacity, perfecting their skills in their trade, profession or occupation, and making a contribution to the wellbeing of the whole society, they are judged by criteria which have nothing to do with the human dimensions of work, apart from the earning of a salary and the contribution to making profit for the company. Cooperation and emotional intelligence are tools in the art of getting your own way. Political correctness and philanthropy are likewise "reputation-management tools, strategic tools to build brand loyalty", as I read recently in the advertising for a management training company. This is identified as "outcome-based giving" i.e. giving with an ulterior motive.

- Politics is all about the balanced budget, the highest GDP (Gross Domestic Product) and parity with the dollar. The "body of persons authorized to administer the laws, or to govern a state" lose sight of their function to provide a safe and caring society, nurturing the potential of all people within it. Again, the human dimension is lost in the service of the great god, Wealth. Politicians themselves spend their time fighting with each other to gain most attention, and court most votes. The tactics used are those of the gutter-press and the political-media—slurring and muck-raking—as common civility is lost in the fiercely competitive battle zone of local and national politics.

What about human values? Where are they in the vast competitive machinery of intellectual and monetary brilliance? Modern psychological research has conclusively demonstrated that we are motivated by more than just monetary gain. Once we reach a reasonable level of material comfort, more money doesn't necessarily increase our happiness. We all need sustenance and security, and the dignity of work, but we get our greatest satisfaction from making a difference or making a contribution to the greater good—we gain the most self-esteem and pleasure from being able to help others.

2. A Paradigm Shift

The overall aim of this work is to *encourage action by everyone*, by demonstrating that change is possible without "re-inventing the wheel" or significant expenditure. It's not about experts, who understand the jargon of economics, and we don't need to demolish any of the organisational structures we have established. We just need to look at them with fresh eyes, and think of how effective their processes are in achieving what we want to achieve.

A paradigm is a conceptual framework within which theories are constructed. The ideas of *wealth creation* and *wealth accumulation* are an extension of the human functions of food production, gathering and storage, which grew into the industrial functions of the production, distribution and consumption of goods and services. The paradigm of *Wealth* is a bi-product of the application of human ingenuity to the resources of the world. It's about efficiency of scale—as the population grew, we needed to think about more efficient ways to manage resources. We need wealth to nurture life and thrive—we just need to think carefully about what we *all* need from it, and how much of it we each need. We can no longer continue with a model where 10% of the population holds 90% of the wealth, and many of the other 90% are struggling to survive.

Mankind created money and the idea of wealth to be the servant of mankind, and we have inadvertently allowed the servant to become the master—having created the rod for our own backs, we now service the archetype of our own creation and bow to a vast industry of wealth creators, all with a vested interest in keeping the system going. Like the pyramids of Egypt, the energy of whole nations is harnessed to build the monuments within empires dedicated to Wealth. The "priests" of the system are those who have a vested interest in maintaining the status quo, since it is how they earn their living, but it may not be in the greater interest of the majority to continue "building the pyramids of power and wealth".

An archetype, according to Carl Jung, is the manifestation of a central idea, which can appear in an image or a thought, but its function is to organise behaviour. The paradigm is then embedded into our psyche, individual and collective, and its roots go deep. It becomes hidden in our unconscious, but all of our creative energy is used to fulfil it. The pyramids were built to epitomise the idea of eternal life and life after death, and much of the wealth and human energy of Egypt was eventually funnelled into these efforts, to the detriment of the living kingdom. Today, the monuments to this folly still stand, but the glory which was ancient Egypt is long dead—a new Egypt is in the process of being born, hopefully in the image of a modern democracy, which exemplifies the rule of people by caring people, with social justice for all of the people.

If *Wealth* is our paradigm or archetype of choice, the whole architecture of our society reflects that choice. If *"Creating wealth for individuals and nations"* is the message we constantly "feed" people, the resulting behaviour is acquisition, greed, cheating and fighting over natural resources. If we make our pivotal idea *"Creating a hopeful future by nurturing people and the environment",* the behaviour we encourage is sharing, caring, cooperation and preserving the world's resources—we are focusing on creating a future of peace as our legacy for our children. By focusing on the new *Democracy Trifecta of People, Relationships and Infrastructure,* we are able to take a fresh look at our priorities.

3. Focusing on a More Hopeful Future

We are a creative species, and we have created the organisational structures and networks of education, business and government to increase the efficiency with which we harness and share resources, physical, intellectual, emotional and spiritual. The history of the development of these universal responses to resource harvesting and distribution sheds light on how we might re-focus our attention to create a better world society:

- Education is about *learning how to learn creatively*, by developing body, mind and spirit. It is about much more than performance. Lifelong learning is a necessity in our fast-changing world.

- Business is about *organising work*, for the benefit of all. It is about much more than profit. Everyone needs the dignity of work and the opportunity to contribute to society in a meaningful way.

- Government is about *coordinating our efforts and resources* on a community and worldwide basis to maximise our potential for peace and prosperity. It is about much more than politics. Governments need to put people first and foster more meaningful relationships between all sectors of society.

I believe that the structures we have created are efficient responses and archetypal in form—there is no need to dismantle the essential frameworks. What is required is a re-focusing of our perception of their purpose and a rethinking of the values they reflect. The language of the factory—process and product; fixed framework and structure; quality assurance and performance indicators—might be replaced by the language of *flexible design and reflective process*, focusing on the evolving and creative nature of the intended outcome.

Values are visible through the actions people take, not their talk:

- If you value integrity, you tell the truth.
- If you value equality, you control the physical trappings of power, status and inequality.
- If you value people, you take care of them.

I challenge you to create a more hopeful future, using existing organisational structures. The means at your disposal are your creative intelligence and your experience base. The world is a complex place, but we each have knowledge and strengths which we can bring to the design table. Fresh thinking about the ideas which inspired education, business and government is provided by ancient and contemporary creative thinkers.

This is a book about *Creative Learning*—how we learn; why we learn; and how we can learn better. I believe that learning is the central process of life, and that what we focus on determines what we learn and how we behave. Learning is about finding out how to *survive*, and then how to *thrive*. Creative intelligence is the conscious desire to understand the environment, using curiosity, reason, intuition and wisdom, and then applying that knowledge and understanding to solve life's problems.

All humans have a natural capacity for learning on personal, social and political levels—we all negotiate with each other and with our environment to survive. We start out naturally selfish—we need sustenance and shelter and we need someone to give us these things. We are born helpless and we learn self-assertiveness in order to become independent. Later, we learn that we are part of a family, a group, a community—we learn self-consciousness and cooperation at the same time, as we strive to achieve self-esteem, success and significance.

We all enjoy attention, and we are a social species—friendship and relationship are fundamental to our happiness. We learn that selfishness is not a good basis for friendship. As we progress in consciousness, we hopefully reach the stage of self-realisation, where we achieve success and fulfil our personal ambitions.

The connection between spiritually evolved world figures like Moses, Buddha, Jesus, Muhammad, Ghandi and Martin Luther King Jr is that they succeeded in conveying a universal message for change—they attained Unity Consciousness, recognising that our highest achievement is to care for each other in a tolerant society which embraces difference.

4. Changing the World by Changing Our Focus

The following extract from the Humanist Manifesto III, whose signatories included 21 Nobel laureates, outlines ethical values which are universal, and can be embraced by people of all religions and none as a way forward to identify core principles which we can all accept to guide our relationships, local and international. They are values without borders:

- *Ethical values are derived from human need and interest as tested by experience.*

- *Life's fulfillment emerges from individual participation in the service of humane ideals.*

- *Humans are social by nature and find meaning in relationships.*

- *Working to benefit society maximizes individual happiness.*

My purpose in writing this book and the *Creative Learning Series* is to encourage everyone to think about how we can change the things we want to improve. I want to make a difference to how we think and to empower everyone to play a part in initiating change by finding a confident voice and exercising full citizen's rights to nurture life— key elements in this change are *inclusion* and *participation*.

We start by changing our local communities, to make them more inclusive and nurturing. In the wider world, we urgently need to reach consensus to bring peace to the ongoing Clash of Civilisations. We can no longer rely on the pivotal ideal of *"wealth as the securing of scarce resources"*, which galvanised individual competing states in the past—our world is much smaller, and our technologies more powerful, so that the devastating effects of modern mistakes are much more significantly detrimental on a global scale.

If we choose a single idea which enables us to reach consensus, and to retain and enjoy the variety and diversity of our cultures, we may manage to move forward on a positive footing. Whatever we choose, it has to be something which everyone can agree to and simple enough for anyone to learn—something we can all remember and act upon as often as possible. We need to change our mindset—personal, social and international.

This is my proposal for the affirmation which will change our focus and change our world:

We will create a more hopeful future by nurturing people and the environment.

Before you smile cynically about the naivety of this proposal, consider this—every human being shows kindness to some living creature. It may not be much, but even Adolph Hitler showed affection to his dog. Appealing to the ethical conscience of even the most hardened military or religious leader is a necessary step in any lasting international solution. Making a strong ethical statement about what is right behaviour reinforces our understanding of that behaviour—it is an affirmation of our *ethical paradigm as humans*, which transcends borders, race and religion.

We must ensure that repressive regimes become a thing of the past—they are an historical anachronism in our age of social justice. Their time is limited but their leaders hold on to power by fear and isolation, violently quelling attempts at freedom by their people. These violent individuals rule by continual fear and danger of death, and the tool the world community must use is that of the *just war*, waged by the forces of the United Nations as a coalition of peace and social justice—we export security to ensure the health of a society.

It behoves the international community to bring strong pressure to bear on recalcitrant individuals in recalcitrant states, especially those where religiously sanctioned violence exerts a powerful influence. This is impossible on a reactive basis—the atrocities of genocide have happened before the international community can galvanise to intervene, as the recent example of Libya demonstrates.

Change is only possible at the level of the individual—by the time it becomes a "gang response", the effects are devastating. We need to choose a universal affirmation which is simple to remember, and not open to religious or cultural bias—it needs to be something which we say every day, with the power of daily prayer in its ability to change consciousness, and draw us up short if we go astray.

The tribal mentality supported by religious zealotry is the most dangerous threat to international peace in the world today. Tribal arrogance masquerading as religious morality is as prevalent in the West as in the Middle East, and will only be overcome by choosing an ethical position which disallows the behaviour encouraged by the arrogance of tribal posturing. The power of the gang mentality is strong, whether it is applied to a nation or a company—behaviours which would not be condoned if carried out by an individual are somehow sanctioned if carried out collectively.

The conviction of the rightness of one religion over another is a sad carry-over from an age when supremacy relying on violence and exploitation carried international admiration, as well as political and economic reward. It's an argument that can never be proved or won. That this mentality still prevails in many parts of the world is an indictment of our failure as a world community to stand behind our clearly stated moral and ethical requirements for human rights and social justice, which requires all leaders to be held responsible for their actions.

Clearly conveyed public disapproval, backed by international force if necessary, is still our best tool in our goal of a more compassionate world ethos, but as long as we continue to hold to a double standard, combining admiration with disapproval by turn, we will never succeed in turning the ethical tide. The world stage is very similar to the double standard we apply to so-called "stars" of film, music and sport. We shake our heads and smile in amused disapproval at the behaviour of millionaires and royalty, as if they are not held up to the same standards as "ordinary folks". The hypocrisy of our position does nothing to change behaviour. If we applied the same discipline standards in schools, we would be in court for lack of professionalism.

Every civilisation needs a pivotal idea which gives it purpose, direction and meaning. In the Global Community of today's modern world, we need to choose one pivotal idea wisely, and stick to it. What would you choose as your guiding principle for the world? Choose carefully, because what you choose will have an effect on how we all behave, and that in turn will have an effect on all of our futures. We can't change everything, but we can change our personal behaviour—that is totally within our control.

5. Keeping It Simple

Changing the world is everybody's business—we all inhabit a little bit of it, and we have a vested interest in keeping it going, and in improving it. Choosing an idea that we can all get behind, regardless of nationality, race, sex, class, religious beliefs or political opinions is a sensible way to proceed. The essence of good teaching is to keep it simple. If we make things too complicated, we either get confused or we forget what we need to remember.

Two thousand five hundred years ago, the teachings of Siddhartha Gautama, known as Buddha, identified clear, ethical practices which require that we show kindness, self-restraint and tolerance. Two thousand years ago, the teachings of Jesus, known as Christ, were recorded in what is now the New Testament. He also advocated tolerance and self-control, and summed up his teaching in three words:

"Love one another."

Both Siddhartha and Jesus lived in times of great social, economic and political turmoil. War was an everyday experience for everyone in ancient India and Israel, and religion was also a fact of everyday life. Much of the political organization was controlled by the religious authorities, and corruption was rife. People were searching for another way to be. The gods of Ancient Greece and Imperial Rome were amoral, immoral beings, ruled by greed and personal ambition; they, in turn, "ruled" the human population by whim and fancy, using their superior strength and immortality, as well as magic powers, to exact revenge at perceived slights, and to gain ascendancy.

Thanks to the teaching of wise and spiritually evolved people, the ethical consciousness of the modern world is well established and it is not necessary to adhere to a religion in order to follow the Golden Rule:

Treat other people the way you would like them to treat you.

The bigotry of certain religions and denominations, however, is one of the reasons that many people declare themselves atheists or humanists, and in the West, where religious adherence is not generally a social or political requirement, the humanist position is strongly supported. The bigotry of social and political science is no less unfortunate, however, with its demands for conformity to its perception of the way of the world. Wherever the pressure to conform is supported by force, and maintained through fear, whether for religious or political reasons, this state-condoned violence and intolerance goes against international ethical codes, so whether the justification is "scientific" or "religious", the outcome is a significant cause for concern with respect to the possibility of a meaningful dialogue for peace.

If we are to examine the institution of wise governance, it necessarily brings us around to the question of cultural and intellectual intolerance and its repercussions for violent clashes of opinion. There is a need to agree on a common standard for ethical behaviour which is not connected to religious or political preferences. Just as economics is not an ideology, so science and religion are non-negotiable preferences about ways of considering cultural frameworks and processes. Global communication will overcome rule by disconnection and misinformation, but people who seek to join the world community will continue to need help to break the chains of repression.

As fellow human beings, this is our duty and our responsibility—historically, someone did it for us, and we are "gifting kindness forward." We need to find common ground, and that can only be found in a *culture-neutral ideology* which identifies acceptable ethical behaviour. Continuing to insist that we adhere to common beliefs can only result in a no-win continuation of the present impasse—conversion is not an option, and it's disrespectful to denigrate another person's beliefs just because they don't agree with you, scientist or theologian, believer or humanist. Right behaviour is the standard for judgement, not right belief.

 I think we can agree that most people like to be treated with respect and kindness—there may be a few exceptions to this, but these would be aberrations from the norm. If we were to universally choose to do one thing differently, I think it would be to remember to be kind. I like the slogan:

Commit random acts of kindness.

As Mother Theresa said, in her simple but effective way:

"We shall never know all the good that a simple smile can do."

A smile opens doors, and gladdens hearts. We all enjoy the effect of a simple smile—like kindness, it delivers what all ethical teaching advocates. Hospitality is the practice of welcoming people into your home; charity is helping people who need help, regardless of who they are; to smile at someone is to indicate that you are noticing them, and that you intend to treat them with courtesy, respect and kindness.

6. Playing Your Part

Changing the world seems like an overwhelming task, but it starts with very simple steps. We start the system of change by stepping back from our traditional and routine assumptions of "how things have always been", and asking specific questions about how we would like them to become. This open-minded attitude is the one I hope you will manage to retain as you read on.

The aim of this review of some of Life's most important lessons is to try to achieve a position where we optimise the potential of everyone, and, in particular, our State Institutions of Education, Business and Government to provide prosperity and happiness for their own individual citizens and communities, but ultimately to assist in achieving the goals adopted by the United Nations from the 1941 *State of the Union Address* delivered by US President Franklin Roosevelt as the "essential Four Freedoms":

1. Freedom of speech
2. Freedom of belief
3. Freedom from fear
4. Freedom from want

In today's world, we can no longer assume that we have the luxury of time to address these crucial issues, that the solving of them is someone else's job, or that we can continue to pursue individual or nation-state issues in isolation and competition.

We are already dealing with the threat of international terrorism, and its effect on our freedoms. This is coupled with the looming environmental issues concerning scarcities and pollution, as well as the possible effects of global climate change. We can't assume that world political and religious leaders are the only people who need to lay aside their prejudices and power struggles to achieve genuine consensus.

We all have a part to play in the solution. We can start with where we are, in our communities. We can make a difference at a local level, in our schools, workplaces and political organisations, by thinking carefully about how we behave towards each other. By changing one thing, it is possible to change everything. It starts with you.

PART THREE

How Did We Get Here?

Three Lessons from the Past

When we know how we got to where we are now, we can plan how we are going to change. This part of our *Evolving Strong Democracy* strategy is designed to put things in context, starting with how the development of Democracy is a reflection of our stage of consciousness development.

LESSON ONE

The Growth of Consciousness

"There is nothing that makes men rich and strong but that which they carry inside of them. Wealth is of the heart not of the hand."
John Milton

1. It Started With Religion

The institutions of our world are organisations which reflect our psychological mindset. The earliest forms of cooperative large-scale enterprises were religious—quite apart from the spiritual aspects of individual religious experiences, organised religion is one way of formalising our perception of what is ideal in our world, our aspiration to wholeness, love and connection. It is also a significant means of social cohesion.

All ancient societies developed organised religion, focussed on gods or God, and these evolved, by various routes, into institutions which represent the formal organisation of education, business and government—schools, colleges, universities, offices, stores, factories and parliaments.

The processes of these organisations are what concern us here—how they and we interact, because we have created them and they are there to ensure that our best interests are served. The ethics, values, motivations and behaviour of a person, an organisation, or a culture reflect their stage of development in consciousness, and there are various ways of looking at the progress of consciousness.

2. Human Consciousness and Evolution

With respect to human consciousness and evolution, we might describe evolution as the process whereby conscious existence emerges out of the unconscious gradually, through the stages of matter, life and minds:

1. Matter evolves from simple to complex forms.

2. Life emerges in matter and evolves from simple to complex forms.

3. Mind emerges in life and evolves from rudimentary to higher forms of thought and reason.

As each new principle emerges, the previous stages remain but are integrated into a higher principle. Humanity represents the stage of development of mind in complex material forms of life, but reason and intellect still do not dominate the life of most human beings. Mind tends initially to be used for the purposes of the life principle in a selfish way:

1. Self-preservation

2. Self-assertion

3. Satisfaction of personal needs and desires (the cycle of aversion and desire).

Evolution proceeds with the development of reason and intellect, and the development of caring and compassion. Creative Learning is active and meaningful. It can be an individual pursuing a dream, or people helping each other, as in collaborative learning. All have a need and a right to be involved with one another in mutual learning. This is the meaning of communication—learning from each other in a community, where the community can be local and immediate or international and long-term.

The key is *mutual respect* and *recognition of equal value.* Elitism, hierarchy, prejudice and intolerance leave no room for independence of mind and human compassion. Our aim in learning is always "betterment"—ideally, to make things better for everyone, not at the expense of some. Our history as humans, however, is one of exploitation—of the world's resources and of other humans. Colonisation is the exploitation of other lands and peoples for their resources—slavery is the exploitation of fellow humans for their energy.

3. Becoming More Responsible

Active Citizenship is to take full responsibility for your happiness and success, but to do so without exploitation of others. In fact, it is to recognise the value of cooperation over competition. Good Citizenship is to realise that to take responsibility is more satisfying than to pass it on to others. Community action is "by the people, for the people", and community involvement brings the individual power over his life, enabling him/her to gain confidence through service and mutual benefit.

Throughout time, Man's ideals have been focused towards creating a better society, with more compassion, more love. The means to this end is Education, not in any narrow sense of "going to school to be educated", but in the broadest sense of "learning to be more human". Education means "to lead out"—helping us to discover the best we are capable of, and then enabling us to realise our potential, as individuals, and collectively, as humanity:

- *Religion* was man's earliest form of education, when he tried to emulate what he could imagine, at that stage in his development, as most perfect. *Religio* means "to bind" and religion bound people together in a common belief. Like everything else, religion has to evolve.

- *Philosophy*, which translates from the Greek as the "Love of Wisdom", developed from religion, as man's consciousness developed, and he took more responsibility for the outcome of his choices, no longer blaming his fate on the gods.

- *Science* is what we now call man's exploration of all of the aspects of creation, in order to understand how things work, and how we can use the energy of creation to create a better world.

Each of these disciplines, religion, philosophy and science, might be seen as signifying a stage of development in consciousness, from dependence and subservience, to independence and responsibility, and, at first, they were seen as mutually exclusive.

 We now know that each stage of development overtakes yet includes the previous stage, but at a higher level of understanding. So, when we gain a philosophical understanding, we understand religion in a different way. Likewise with science—when we gain a scientific understanding of the world, our philosophy of life, and our understanding of the meaning of religion, each change to a higher level.

The Greek philosophers, however, judged that belief in the Gods was intellectually "primitive", and refused to give credence to the need of some people to *anthropomorphise* certain concepts in order to use the metaphors to influence behaviour. This attitude was passed down through the ages, to be adopted by the scientists of the Renaissance, ultimately resulting in the *Atheism* of the nineteenth century.

The controversy over Creationism and Evolution which raged at the end of the nineteenth, and into the twentieth century, had its roots in this intellectual difference of opinion. That, coupled with the need to break free from the intellectual strangle-hold of orthodox church dogma, which refused to consider scientific free-thinking, and the stage was set for a schism which continues to this day.

4. Progressing In Religious Consciousness

Groups which hold to their traditional ways, where particular religious ideologies are seen as "the only way to be", and religious hierarchies use violence to ensure adherence to beliefs, have a tendency to resent interference in their application of justice within their own society, and see themselves in competition or conflict with other beliefs. The current "clash" between Muslim and Christian groups has its basis in a disagreement between competing fundamentalists, who think their way is the only way, and who want to impose it on the rest of the world.

At the lowest level of consciousness development, the world is an expression of the will-to-live, but *respect for life* has to become the highest principle, or the selfish principle of life at the expense of others becomes the prime driver. The stages of development of religious consciousness might be seen as the development of compassion, and these are reflected in the Bible:

1. Handing down the Law—*"An eye for an eye; a tooth for a tooth."*— Moses and the Old Testament.

2. Making strict rules—*"Whoever refuses to work is not allowed to eat."*—St Paul in the New Testament.

3. Advocating compassion and leading by example—*"Love one another...Treat your neighbour as yourself."*—Jesus.

5. The Development of Political Consciousness

Much simplified, the history of political development might look like this:

1. **Conquest**—conquering people established themselves, legally and economically, as the privileged class, seized a monopoly of land ownership, and appointed their own ranks to positions of power in government and education, creating class divisions and limiting access to education and positions of power.

2. **Socialism and Capitalism**—public and direct worker ownership, and administration of the means of production and allocation of resources, gives way to equal access to resources for all individuals with a method of compensation based on the amount of labour expended.

    Most socialists share the view that capitalism unfairly concentrates power and wealth among a small segment of society that controls capital and derives its wealth through exploitation, creates an unequal society, does not provide equal opportunities for everyone to maximize their potential, and does not utilize technology and resources to their maximum potential, nor in the interests of the public.

3. **Social Justice and Creative Communities**—based on creative values, which enhance life for everyone, involving ecological, secular, spiritual, egalitarian values; voluntary simplicity; interpersonal growth; self-determination; and democratic/consensus decision-making.

LESSON TWO

Revolution and Wealth Creation

"Riches come in many forms, and most of them have absolutely nothing to do with money."
Carey Martin

1. The Industrial Revolution

Where we are now owes much to the history of the last two hundred and fifty years, as humans have adjusted to the changes of the Industrial Age. Starting in Britain in the middle of the eighteenth century, the Industrial Revolution transformed the world and the way in which millions of people lived. Its effects were more revolutionary than any other development in human history since the discovery of agriculture more than five thousand years ago.

The Industrial Revolution created the way in which most people in the developed world now live—in cities rather than villages, relying for almost all their everyday necessities not on what they or their neighbours can grow or make for themselves, but on large and intricate organisations, staffed by people they will never know or see.

It started in Britain, when a handful of enterprising businessmen and engineers discovered new ways of harnessing water and later steam power and of organising work forces. By the mid nineteenth century, it had transformed British society, and quickly spread to Europe and the United States. Since World War Two, industrialisation has swept the globe, and it is still with us, still changing the lives of people in all parts of the world, bringing great profits to the lucky or enterprising few, and misery and upheaval to many others.

The blessings are mixed, but it has raised living standards enormously, although these advantages have taken a long time to materialise. Up until the outbreak of World War One in 1914, those who benefited most were the rapidly growing middle class and skilled workers. Production and consumption, art and education, leisure and crime, religion and politics—none would escape the transformation that industry brought in its train.

As well as people, it affected the landscape and environment, too, particularly in the decline in the number of people who earned their living by agriculture—from 80% or more in the majority of countries in the eighteenth century to under 5% in many countries today. The close association with the earth and the cultivation and care of plants and animals which had dominated human existence for millennia was brought to an end. The countryside became a sparsely populated but highly efficient food factory, a source of nostalgia but no longer a source of livelihood

2. The Age of Reason

The eighteenth century is known as the Age of Reason or the Enlightenment, and saw a flourishing of intellectual, scientific and cultural life, with reason being advocated as the primary source for legitimacy and authority among significant groups of intellectuals throughout Europe and America, most of whom knew each other personally through the university system. In France, Great Britain, Germany, the Netherlands, Italy, Spain, Portugal and the American Colonies, a spirit of unrest and freedom was in the air. Internationally, its major figures included Diderot, Hume, Kant, Locke, Rousseau and Voltaire.

Natural Law theories challenged the divine right of kings with an alternative justification for the establishment of social contract, positive law and government in the form of classical republicanism. Natural Rights were promoted by these intellectuals—inalienable rights which were described as self-evident and universal, and not contingent upon the laws, customs or beliefs of any particular culture or government. As well as promoting rational scientific enquiry, the Enlightenment thinkers advocated religious tolerance, social reform, progress and the elimination of tyranny. Their great cohesive strength was the formation of clubs, which met on a regular basis to compare ideas, and share thoughts.

A group of very influential friends in Edinburgh included Adam Smith (1723–1790), economist and moral philosopher; David Hume (1711–1776), philosopher, historian and economist, known especially for Empiricism and Scepticism; Frances Hutchison (1694–1746), Presbyterian minister and Chair of Moral Philosophy at the University of Glasgow, where he had been tutor to Adam Smith; Joseph Black (1728–1799), physicist and chemist, Professor of Medicine at the University of Glasgow, who discovered latent heat, specific heat and carbon dioxide, and who conducted experiments on steam-powered engines with James Watt; and James Hutton (1726–1797), geologist, physician, naturalist, chemist and experimental farmer, the Father of Modern Geology, who described Deep Time, presenting a significant challenge to the Church, with its specific timetable of events since the creation—around 4000 years before!

This formidable circle were all founders of the Scottish Enlightenment, and met regularly at the "Poker Club", a cover name for the Militia Club, whose purpose was to reinstate the Scottish Militia for "the dignity of the nation". The militia had been forbidden by the English after the defeat of the Scots in the Stuart Rebellion. With close ties to France and America, their ideas were part of the sweeping changes which led to the American Revolution and the French Revolution.

Having witnessed the devastation in Scotland from the Rebellion of 1745, when Bonnie Prince Charlie rallied an army to reinstate the Stewart monarchy in London, only to end in defeat and the degradation of the Scottish Highlands in particular, these intellectuals, closely connected with both Glasgow and Edinburgh universities, set forth to change the world. Their publications included *Treatise on Human Nature, A History of Natural or Inalienable Rights, The Wealth of Nations, Theory of the Earth, and The Theory of Moral Sentiments.*

3. The Wealth of Nations

In 1776, Adam Smith, Scottish Economist and Moral Philosopher, published *The Wealth of Nations*; and the newly formed American congress published the *Declaration of Independence. The Wealth of Nations* is considered to be the foundation of modern economic theory, and has continued to influence authors, economists, governments and business organisations since it was published.

"As every individual…neither intends to promote the public interest, nor knows how much he is promoting it…he intends only his own security…he intends only his own gain, and he is in this, as in many other cases, led by an invisible hand to promote an end which was no part of his intention. Nor is it always the worse for the society that it was no part of it. By pursuing his own interest he frequently promotes that of the society more effectually than when he really intends to promote it."
Adam Smith
The Wealth of Nations (1776)

Adam Smith's *Wealth of Nations* is often cited as the foundation text for the benefits of freedom to trade, but, to be fair to Adam Smith, his work has been subject to very selective reading by staunch advocates of free trade and de-regulation, who are careful not to draw attention to Adam's statements about taxing the rich, and government's role in controlling their excesses. He also warns government of its duty to protect ordinary working people:

"…labouring poor, that is, the great body of the people who will suffer unless government takes some pains to prevent it…The necessities of life occasion the great expense of the poor. They find it difficult to get food, and the greater part of their little revenue is spent getting it. The luxuries and vanities of life occasion the principal expense of the rich, and a magnificent house embellishes and sets off to the best advantage all the other luxuries and vanities which they possess. A tax on house rents, therefore, would in general fall heaviest on the rich…It is not very unreasonable that the rich should contribute to the public expense, not only in proportion to their revenue, but something more than in that proportion."

Adam Smith was a canny Scot, a modest man, who passionately wanted to make things better for the poor. He was born in Kirkcaldy, in Scotland (as I was), and his father died when he was young. His friends were all social reformers, living in Scotland in the period after the 1745 Stuart Rebellion, the aftermath of which was brutal and merciless.

The members of Adam Smith's intellectual circle were themselves leaders of a social revolution which is still with us, and all of them wanted working people to be self-determining. In the mid-eighteenth century, that could only mean being an artisan, and controlling your own destiny by making money. The people who had made a living from the land had been evicted, and many of them would make their way to America, the land of the free, where there was the chance of a fresh start, free land, and relief from persecution, religious and racial.

4. All Men Are Created Equal

The British colonies in America had a history of individual thought well before the Declaration of Independence of 1776. William Penn (1644–1718) was a real estate entrepreneur, philosopher and founder of the Province of Pennsylvania, and an early champion of democracy and religious freedom.

"*All men are created equal*" is probably the best known phrase in any political document—Thomas Jefferson used the phrase in the Declaration of Independence, as a rebuttal to the Divine Right of Kings. The "*Unalienable Rights*" to "*Life, Liberty and the Pursuit of Happiness*", and the duty of Government to secure these rights for all people, also written into the Declaration, were also conditional, however—in 1776, not everyone had these rights. Only those, and such-as-those, were seen as having the right to liberty and happiness.

The idea of Democracy was born in ancient Greece, but only *free men* had the right to participate in the governance of the state. Women and slaves, who together made up the majority of the population, had *no rights of property or person under the law*. Slavery was not outlawed in the British Empire until 1833, and slaves were not emancipated in the USA until 1865, by President Lincoln, 89 years after the Declaration of Independence had declared that all men were created equal.

In fact, the Declaration was very specific in its references. It meant only to specify that certain landowners, property owners and business owners in America were equal to landowners, property owners and business owners in Great Britain, and would not have their right to make profit curtailed in any way by being subject to the British Crown in the form of a colony, subject to taxation, and having no rights to free trade. The Crown and its agents had a monopoly on all trade from the British colonies throughout the world.

Of course, writing this in the Declaration of Independence would not have had the same ring as "*All men are created equal*". Then, as now, our ideals are one thing, and all too often, our actions are another. Our ideals are wonderful things—they are the initial idea, sparked by our best self, but they require to be worked out in reality. The elements require constant examination to ensure that they are actually realized. Then they must be kept under review, to ensure that they are not eroded by time and circumstance.

Women could not vote in Britain until the first half of the twentieth century, and people of colour continued to be discriminated against and could not vote in the USA until well into the second half of the twentieth century, so the ideas and ideals which we espouse are all relative with respect to our behaviour.

5. The Scottish-American Billionaire –
Andrew Carnegie

Andrew Carnegie (1835–1919), the Scottish-American industrialist, businessman, entrepreneur and major philanthropist was born in Dunfermline, Scotland (barely ten miles from the birth place of Adam Smith), and migrated to the United States as a child with his parents. His father was a weaver, and starting as a worker in a bobbin factory, Andrew's success came from being in the right place at the right time, and his natural business acumen.

In 1853, he was employed by Thomas A Scott of the Pennsylvania Railroad Company as a secretary/telegraph operator, progressing rapidly through the company, to become superintendent of the Pittsburgh division. Railroads were big business, and Pittsburgh, Pennsylvania was one of the biggest. Scott helped him with investments which depended on insider knowledge—he invested in railroads, iron, bridges and rails. The Civil War brought further opportunities for transportation and munitions, and Pittsburgh became a centre of wartime production. Andrew and other investors established a steel rolling mill, later expanding into all aspects of the iron and steel industry.

He had good business sense, charm and literary knowledge—books and libraries were an important part of Andrew's life, beginning with his childhood in Scotland, where he listened to readings and discussions from books from the Tradesmen's Subscription Library, which his father, a handloom weaver, had helped to create. He later borrowed books from the personal library of Colonel James Anderson, who opened his collection to his workers every Saturday, as Carnegie noted in his autobiography.

Andrew Carnegie built Pittsburgh's Carnegie Steel Company, later to become US Steel, and also Carnegie Hall in Manhattan, New York, one of the most prestigious venues in the world for music of all kinds. He turned to philanthropy and education, founding the Carnegie Corporation of New York, the Carnegie Endowment for international Peace, and many other educational establishments.

In 1889, aged 54, Carnegie wrote an essay entitled, *"Wealth"*, more commonly known as *"The Gospel of Wealth"*, which described the responsibility for philanthropy by the new upper class of self-made rich. The central thesis of Carnegie's essay was the peril of allowing large sums of money to be passed into the hands of persons or organizations ill-equipped mentally or emotionally to cope with them— the wealthy entrepreneur must take responsibility for distributing his fortune so that it would be put to good use, and not wasted on frivolous expenditure.

Andrew disapproved of charitable giving that did not create opportunities for the beneficiaries to better themselves. He believed that the dependants of the rich and privileged should be supported in moderation, with the bulk of the wealth being used to enrich the community. He advocated high taxation of estates on a progressive scale, with moderate sums to dependants "until all of the millionaire's hoard, at least the other half, comes to the privy coffer of the State."

He endowed public libraries, called Carnegie Libraries, in cities and towns throughout the US, and as far afield as Britain, Canada, Australia, New Zealand, Serbia, the Caribbean and Fiji—2509 were funded between 1883 and 1929, the first being built in his hometown of Dunfermline in Scotland in 1883, a sandstone building with the motto *"Let there be light"* at the entrance.

Andrew's personal experience as an immigrant who, with the help of others, worked his way into a position of wealth, reinforced his ideas of a society based on merit, where anyone who worked hard could become successful, coupled with philanthropy, where the successful had a duty to help others. He was quite specific about who he thought "deserved" help however. He believed in giving to the "industrious and ambitious, not those who need everything done for them, but those who, being most anxious and able to help themselves, deserve and will be benefited by help from others".

"The Carnegie Formula" for libraries required certain conditions to be fulfilled by the town:

- Demonstrate the need for a public library

- Provide the building site
- Annually provide 10% of the cost of the library's construction to support its operation and
- Provide free service for all

One of the requirements was for the willingness of the people and government to raise taxes to support the library—the design of the libraries, with self-service shelves, enabling people to browse and choose, was a significant reason for their success.

When he realized that he could not give away all of his fortune within his lifetime, Carnegie established the Carnegie Foundation to continue his programme of giving. Andrew Carnegie is regarded as the second richest man in history after J D Rockefeller. He sold the Carnegie Steel Company in 1901 for $480 million to J P Morgan, who created US Steel. Andrew was sixty-five years old and he devoted the next eighteen years of his life to large-scale philanthropy, with a specific emphasis on local libraries, world peace, education and scientific research. The work of the Carnegie Foundation continues today.

From the beginning, Andrew Carnegie believed in using his fortune for others and doing more than "making money". At age thirty-three he wrote:

"I propose to take an income no greater than $50,000 per annum. Beyond this I need never earn, make no effort to increase my fortune, but spend the surplus each year for benevolent purposes. Let us cast aside business forever, except for others…Man must have an idol and the amassing of wealth is one of the worst species of idolatry!"

Andrew Carnegie was clear that his wealth was to be used to create a hopeful future for generations to come, and that that would be achieved by encouraging learning.

6. The American Billionaire – Henry Ford

Henry Ford (1863-1947) was another billionaire who changed the face of industry throughout the world with his efficient method of assembling cars. He founded the Ford Motor Company, which pioneered assembly-line production, driving down costs and making automobile ownership a staple feature of American life. "The production line" became a catch-phrase for factories and the method spread throughout the world.

Henry by all accounts was a hard task-master, but he understood how to make cars and make money:

Coming together is the beginning
Keeping together is progress
Working together is success
Henry Ford

He had a highly idiosyncratic style of charitable giving. He saw work as the purpose of human existence, and he deeply disliked anything that seemed to undermine its discipline, especially something as well intentioned as philanthropy. He distrusted organized charities, although he created quite a few himself. Despite his stated misgivings, Ford seems to have dedicated about one-third of his income to philanthropy.

Henry was born on a Michigan farm in July 1863, and he absorbed the farmer's tireless work ethic, but hated agriculture. His father was an Irish immigrant, who left Ireland in 1847 during the potato famine. His mother, Mary Litogot O'Hearn was an orphan adopted by the O'Hearn family. William and Mary met while he worked at her family's farm. Mary died in childbirth when Henry was twelve. His father, seeing that the boy was distraught, gave him a watch to distract him, knowing that Henry would take it apart. Sure enough, he did, using his mother's pins as tools, little knowing that this skill would help him in his first job in Detroit, repairing watches!

He was brilliant mechanically, and as a boy, he would strip down and reassemble any machine he could lay his hands on. (He sounds like my husband.) "Every clock in the Ford house shudders when it sees Henry coming," a friend is said to have quipped. At sixteen, he left the farm for Detroit, and found work first as a watch repairer, then a machinist and later as an engineer. By the time he was thirty-nine, he had founded two car companies, both of which failed, yet he was undeterred.

In 1903, he borrowed $28,000 to found the Ford Motor Company, and the early cars produced made enough profit to make him very wealthy, wealthy enough to take on the pioneering Model T project. When the first car rolled off the assembly line in October 1908, the Model T revolutionized the automobile industry. In ruthless pursuit of efficiency gains, Henry Ford had pioneered unprecedented production methods. He used machine-made, standardized parts, which were put together along a continuously moving assembly line. This allowed him to sell the Model T at a profit for $345, when other cars sold for $1000. Orders poured in and eventually over 15 million Model Ts were sold.

By the mid-1920s, his net worth was a staggering $1.2 billion, yet Ford was not interested particularly in money and what it could buy. In average years, he gave away 33 percent of his income, when, by comparison, most people in his earnings bracket gave away 5 percent. What Ford himself considered to be genuine philanthropy were small gifts to help individuals, of which he gave many. He gave away money, food, automobiles and other articles, where he could see a need and thought it would give the person a leg-up. He believed that charitable giving should be *"a private and individual act"*, one that was *"spontaneous on the part of the giver, unanticipated and unsought by the beneficiary and a generous gesture without any element of calculation."*

He launched a few philanthropic projects of his own. In 1911, he and his wife created Valley Farm, an 80-acre home for orphan boys. During the First World War, he housed Belgian war refugees. He built a trade school in Detroit and a school for African Americans in Georgia. During the Great Depression he paid for two work camps for boys. The Henry Ford Hospital in Detroit was paid for by Ford and during his lifetime he donated over $14 million, and to this day, it remains one of Detroit's largest hospitals. He wanted the hospital to reflect his philosophy of work and self-reliance, and the patients were working men and their families. He subsidized some of the costs of the medical care, but took pains to ensure that patients would contribute. *"There are plenty of hospitals for the rich,"* Ford explained. *"There are plenty of hospitals for the poor. There are no hospitals for those who can afford to pay only a moderate amount yet desire to pay without a feeling that they are recipients of charity."*

Henry's personal passion was historical preservation. He restored his family's homestead in Dearborn in 1919, and then he restored the Wayside Inn, near Sudbury, Massachusetts, a tavern celebrated in verse by Henry Wadsworth Longfellow. To enhance the property, he bought up surrounding buildings and restored them too, at a total cost of $15million. He was a lifelong collector of Americana, and in 1926, decided to house his collection at Dearborn. For over twenty years, Henry had collected everything he could find – from locomotives, to fabric to historic buildings – including the courthouse where Abraham Lincoln practised law, and the Wright Brother's bicycle shop- and had them shipped to Dearborn. The entire collection was opened in October 1929 by President Hoover, and remains one of America's great living-history museums, known as Greenfield Village.

Henry Ford's life spanned the steam engine to the jet engine, from 1863 to 1947, and he himself was a large part of the technological revolution. He did a lot of good for humankind through his work, but his philosophy was one of rugged individualism. He believed in *"a hand up not a hand-out"*. The Ford Foundation is Henry Ford's lasting legacy, and one of its earliest grants was to help start up the Public Broadcasting Service (PBS), which provides educational programming for adults and children. The foundation has four key goals:
1. Strengthen democratic values.
2. Reduce poverty and injustice.
3. Promote international cooperation.

4. Advance human achievement.

It works to achieve these goals through three funding areas:
1. Asset building and community development.
2. Peace and social justice, including human rights and
    governance and civil society.
3. Knowledge, creativity and freedom, including education,
    sexuality, religion, media, arts and culture.

These two great men of the late Industrial Age, Andrew Carnegie and
Henry Ford, shared many qualities. They were both self-made men,
rugged and ruthless pioneers of the Modern Industrial Society. They
valued hard work and encouraged it in others. They were worried
about society becoming too soft, yet they had concern for the weak
and the poor. Their contradictions are those we all share and the
Democratic Spirit is one which seeks to help everyone to become self-
sufficient and self-determining as far as they are able. They each were
men of purpose and passion, and they made a huge impression on the
whole world which remains today. They were Industrial Giants.

*"The moment human helplessness is systematized, organized, commercialized, and
professionalized, the heart of it is extinguished, and it becomes a cold and clammy
thing."*
Henry Ford

LESSON THREE

Public Welfare and Power Elites

"If you have nothing else to do, look about you and see if there isn't something close at hand that you can improve! It may make you wealthy, though it is more likely to make you happy."
George Matthew Adams

1. The Power of the Collective

Albert Schweitzer (1875–1965) theologian, philosopher and physician, who won the 1952 Nobel Peace Prize for his philosophy, *Reverence for Life,* spent his life in the passionate quest to discover a universal ethical philosophy anchored in a universal reality, and to make it directly available to all of humanity. For him, compassion and service were the keys:

"Until he extends his circle of compassion to include all living things, man will not himself find peace…I don't know what your destiny will be, but one thing I do know: the only ones among you who will be really happy are those who have sought and found how to serve."
Albert Schweitzer

Great thinkers tend to be great doers—Albert Schweitzer, Rudolf Steiner, Albert Einstein, Leonardo da Vinci, Muhammad the Prophet, Jesus the Christ, Gautama the Buddha—creative thinking results in taking action to make things better.

Community is the highest social ideal of humanity, for it is the most efficient and pleasant way to do our work. A community is a group of people who interact with one another—a real, vibrant, living community is a group of people who help one another, who cooperate, who balance the need for privacy with the need for fellowship. Together everyone achieves more.

2. The Power Elite

We should be aware that the power of the group is well understood by what has been called the "Power Elite". In 1956, in the post-World War II era, Charles Wright Mills (1916–1962), American sociologist, and professor at Columbia University, published *The Power Elite,* in which he suggested that the major institutions of modern society were the hierarchies of state, corporation and army, and that in the US, major national power resided in the economic, political and military domains.

Furthermore, the political, military and economic elite, as he described it, shared a common world-view:

- *The military metaphysic:* a military definition of reality
- *Class identity:* recognising themselves as separate and superior to the rest of society
- *Inter-changeability (horizontal mobility)*: they move within and between the three institutional structures and hold interlocking directorates
- *Cooptation/socialization*: socialization of prospective new members is done based on how well they "clone" themselves socially after such elites

According to Mills, the "community of interests" was driven by the "military metaphysics" which had transformed the economy into a "permanent war economy". Dr Philippe Billon, Assistant Professor of Geography at the University of British Columbia describes the "war economy" as a "system of producing, mobilising and allocating resources to sustain violence." Recent events in the world would suggest that there is a sense of continuous war being a possibility, despite the progress that we are making in democratisation and human rights.

That there exists a "power elite" is irrefutable—recent research shows that 80% of the wealth in the US is held by 20% of the population (in line with the Pareto Principle). That these wealthy people tend to know each other, socially, politically and through business is also no surprise, but the extent to which they work collaboratively to achieve common aims is perhaps less well understood.

Michael Mann, Professor of Sociology at the University of California at Los Angeles, wrote Volume I of *The Sources of Social Power* in 1988, and Volume II in 1993. His *IEMP model* states that the power structures within Western civilization are based on the importance given to *four overlapping networks:*

1. *Ideological*—universities and churches are an example of organizations which provide for the collective search for meaning.
2. *Economic*—organizational networks to extract, transform, distribute and consume resources.
3. *Military*—defined in terms of the social organization of physical violence.
4. *Political*—networks with the primary function of territorial regulation, as well as more general regulatory and judicial services—the control of the state.

According the Michael Mann, each form of social power generates its own *vested interest,* which in turn compete and cooperate with each other. He sees the future as an expansion of the global capitalist economy, the nation-state system, wars and ideologies.

3. Social Networking and Controlling Vested Interests

The benefits of the collective, of face-to-face time together, of building something together, of sharing fun, of being part of the group—none of this is underestimated by the power elite. All of the cohesive elements of rules, roles, routines and ritual are employed to good effect, as they are in the fraternity and sorority systems in higher education.

The point is not that there is anything wrong with this social networking system—in fact, it is one of the main factors in successful learning for everyone. All of us need to find a *supportive circle* to enable us to move forward in our development.

The problem for me in the whole notion of power elites is not that they exist—of course there will be rich, powerful people who will work together. It's what they work together for that's the potential problem.

Throughout history, there have been rich and powerful people, men and women, who have sought to do good by using their wealth and energy. They have recognised two things:

1. The gift of intelligence, wealth or skill is just that—a gift. It is not anything to be particularly proud of; it is something to be grateful for.

2. A gift is there to be given and shared. Sharing our gifts with others less fortunate, or enabling others to progress in life, is the best use of our bounty.

Once we have enough personal sustenance, security and significance, we should be able to reach out to others, to help them attain the same level in order to play an appropriate part in the fullness of life.

There will always be a Power Elite—it is the nature of humanity that some are more successful than others.

In the interests of world peace, however, we must be aware that, if there is a mentality there which glorifies war, and which believes that economic success depends on war, we must work together to ensure that the "war mongers" don't prevail. America's supremacy in the modern world, for instance, is purely a matter of economics and military might, and we should beware of focussing on this dimension only—it is a feature of the old mindset, derived from an era of colonisation.

4. Public Welfare and a Life of Dignity.

We constantly struggle with the egalitarian aspects of a democratic society, where *everyone* is entitled to a standard of living compatible with human dignity. Even today, when we are intellectually able to grasp the benefits of free access to education, welfare and health care, we find it difficult to imagine that giving everyone a fair share of these fundamental human rights will not deprive us of our share.

In general, a welfare state is one that provides for the welfare, or well-being, of its citizens, recognizing that as a primary function of government. Such a government is involved in caring for citizens, with the clear and explicit intention of preventing economic hardship and creating dignified human standards of living for all by providing public transport subsidy (including out-with cities), childcare, social amenities, public parks and libraries, as well as many other goods and services designed to enhance human dignity leading to inclusion and self-esteem.

Some of these are paid for via government insurance programmes, while others are paid for by taxes—the aim is to provide a "safety net" designed to help the most vulnerable. All advanced societies view helping people who literally cannot help themselves as decent, humane and necessary.

The reality of providing a good welfare state is challenging—ensuring that people who are capable of looking after themselves do not abuse the system is a difficult task.

On balance, however, the provision of a welfare system which sees citizens leading a dignified life in a caring society far outweighs the few abuses which actually occur. It's no excuse to abdicate responsibility for compassionate government because of the few cases of abuse which happen annually.

In Europe, welfare services are regarded as universal. They are available to rich and poor alike, thus guaranteeing a minimal level of well being and social support for all citizens, without the stigma of charity. The aim is to secure a dignified life for every citizen, and to foster social inclusion.

In the Scandinavian countries of Denmark, Norway and Sweden, taxes are high, but all people enjoy the benefits of a social welfare system which is of a very high quality. These countries are regularly at the top of every index of Wellbeing and Human Happiness.

Canada became a welfare state after the passage of the social welfare reforms in the 1960s, although the social services aspect of the Canadian Welfare State is less developed than in Europe. Many programmes were scaled back in the 1990s as government priorities shifted towards reducing debt and deficit, and Canadian politicians looked more to the US for their trading partnerships.

 The "balanced budget" mentality was about money, not wellbeing, and the result of the policies of the past 20 years in Canada is an erosion of provision, particularly in the health sector, so that recent surveys have placed Canada last amongst British Commonwealth countries with respect to the quality of health provision.

In the US, Welfare has traditionally referred to financial aid for the poor, with more of an emphasis on "charity" than on social inclusion and social justice. The constant back-and-forth between the Democratic and Republican Parties re the support of Public Wellbeing does nothing to create a hopeful future for the millions of Americans who struggle to make ends meet.

The rich and entitled US political elites seem to spend a lot of government time arguing over reducing programmes for citizens' wellbeing, health-care, and education, and about giving the lowest paid working people a living wage, which would get them off welfare. "The rich can get richer and the poor can go to hell," is the message so many hard-working US citizens take from this recurrent display of complacency from their elected representatives.

Exceptional people set a standard for the rest of us to aspire to, but maintaining the commitment to excellence is not easy for the normal politician, often more concerned with getting votes from lobby groups than preserving egalitarian social measures.

If politicians persist in an inward-looking, self-aggrandizing maintenance of the status quo of haves and have-nots, they fail to create a future worth living, where dignity for all is the goal. The demoralisation reinforced by poverty and by endemic deficits in opportunity creates a downward spiral, where hope and faith in a better future are eroded.

A people's aspirations are fired when they see the opportunity to re-engage with a caring community by caring for others themselves. The job of good governance is to *provide security* and *foster* opportunity—welfare is not charity, but the offering of hope for a future worth living and a life of dignity for all.

PART FOUR

Where Do We Go From Here?

The central idea of *The New Democracy Trifecta of People, Relationships and Infrastructure* will guide us as we progress, and frame our considerations of what we need to reconsider to make a difference. The idea here is to explore how we can re-define and re-energize our democracies using the *New Democracy Trifecta* as the framework, to increase personal, socio-economic and environmental wellbeing to benefit everyone.

1. **People** – Personal wellbeing for every citizen.
2. **Relationships** – Socio-economic wellbeing for every society.
3. **Infrastructures** – Environmental wellbeing for the entire world

The values which we teach in schools, and in society as a whole, need to change if we are to create a society in which moderation and concern for others is to become the norm. The spectacle of greed and conspicuous consumption which led to the recent financial crisis, particularly in the United States of America, is nothing to be proud of, yet the perpetrators of that situation were all well educated professionals whose selfish disregard for the consequences of their actions led the whole world into financial chaos.

We must look to our value system and ensure that the learning which we encourage will be directed towards creating families, businesses and communities which espouse the values which will nurture and enliven lives, and where we address the social inequities which exist throughout the world.

These are our challenges, but they are not insurmountable. What we need is some clear thinking about what we hope to get out of our lifelong learning systems, and where we want to get to. When we know where we want to go, we can put in place processes and practices that will get us there. We don't have to start from scratch and we don't have to scrap our schools. We do need to examine our systems with an open mind, and stop practices that are perpetuating disaffection and disassociation. We need to ensure that we have true human values rather than those of the market place in our places of learning.

1. Rethinking Our Value System

The purpose of the evolution of consciousness is to enable new generations to use history to make decisions about values and conduct which benefit the continuity of civilisation. Obligations, memories, hopes and fears are weighed in terms of prevailing value judgements, and decisions are made as to whether to continue with the status quo or change. Noam Chomsky, criticising the way free market principles have been applied, has argued that the wealthy use free-market rhetoric to justify imposing greater economic risk upon the lower classes, while their wealth affords them greater freedom from the vagaries of the market by political and economic advantages

In *Rethinking the Future,* Alvin and Heidi Toffler point out the consequences of the change from the "second wave" society of the industrial revolution (late-18th century to mid-20th century), to the "third wave", post-industrial society.

The industrial society was based on "mass production, mass distribution, mass consumption, mass medication, mass media, mass recreation, mass entertainment, and weapons of mass destruction" combined with "standardization, centralisation, concentration and synchronisation", leading to the style of organisation we call *bureaucracy.*

The post-industrial society is marked by a "scientific-technological revolution, de-massification, diversity, knowledge-based production and the acceleration of change".

"The illiterate of the 21st century will not be those who cannot read and write, but those who cannot learn, unlearn, and relearn."
Alvin Toffler
Rethinking the Future

The roots of the changes we are now experiencing started in the 1950s, the year white-collar workers outnumbered blue-collar workers in the US. The industrial economy based on manual labour was changing over to one based on knowledge or mind-work.

The knowledge based wealth system meant that systems theory, information sciences, software programming, training in project management skills and science and maths emphasis in schools took off, increasing the importance of wealth-relevant knowledge exponentially. The elite schools were the first to grasp the importance of the changes, and the public school systems of the world, by and large, lagged behind.

The changes are now upon us, and we are experiencing significant boundary shifts in existing job markets, as more flexible employment leads to a fall in traditional job opportunities. People no longer have a "job for life", and re-training is the order of the day for many. When this is coupled with the pressure on jobs from emerging countries, with companies relocating to labour markets which are cheaper and less restrictive, in India and Mexico, and the rise of China in world markets, the developed countries are facing considerable economic upheaval in employment patterns.

As economists and governments struggle to understand fully the implications of these changes for local labour markets, the pace of change will not let up. There is an urgent need for education and training to change to more flexible, imaginative and creative processes, and for businesses and employers to provide a supportive network for these changes to take place without undue hardship on individuals and communities.

The education of yesterday, with its need for conformity and its strict subject boundaries, urgently needs to get in the game. Public Private Partnership is not just about money—it's about survival. Neither businesses nor schools can continue to put people last—our people are our strength.

Life is about give and take. When we learn to give generously and to take graciously, we are creating an atmosphere of compassion and caring which fosters civility, and extends dignity to everyone. We all need to earn a living in order to survive, and money is an important facet of our world.

As a means of exchange, its efficiency is unsurpassed, but the temptations of money, fostering avarice and envy, mean that we often have an ambivalent attitude to making our living and being wealthy.

Ethical business practice is part of creating a strong democracy, where success is not a selfish quest, but a means to an end. You realise that by helping yourself, you can help others. Being enterprising and using your gifts to generate wealth gives you a power to help far in excess of what you might do if you have no wealth to share. In *Creative Self-Development,* I set out to demonstrate that self-development is not a selfish thing, but that we have a duty to be the best we can, to fulfil our destiny

There is no use in harking back to the "good old days"—we live in a commercial world, and we enjoy the products and inventions of commerce. To create a compassionate society, we choose an ethical position based on care for each other, and on having enough. Any culture shift needs to extend compassion, consideration, respect and honesty from everyday life to the worlds of education, religion, business and politics.

Mankind must *choose* to create the moral and ethical structures of civilisation: the world-view must derive from the life-view, and we must give priority to volition, to ethical will, as our life view. By focussing on the principles of compassion, we have the potential to create a flexible, adaptable culture, where everyone can play a part, according to his ability, and where no one is left out in the cold world of neglect.

Fundamental changes are urgently required in the values and practices of the dominant world system—our creative and intellectual powers need to devise a way of life which is abundant but not exploitative, where nurturing life is a core value. The change of mindset has already started and the tipping point is approaching. The industrial revolution of the 18th century was a necessary intervention to increase the efficiency with which we produced resources to support a growing population. The agricultural revolution which accompanied it was also necessary—the production of food in a more efficient way allows people to free themselves from unnecessary toil.

The narrow model of laissez-fair capitalism which prioritises growth, gain and profit, which sees humans as machines and nature and living beings as resources to be treated as objects for exploitation and consumption is why we are where we are in experiencing financial crisis, poverty, war and despair. In nature, the lemmings throw themselves off the edge to drown—we surely have more options!

We reap what we sow, in more ways than one, and crisis is the time to review our practices and choose a more humane way—truth, love and beauty are values intrinsic to life, and a dignified human existence requires that we recognise them and give them their rightful place.

There is a need for millionaires and billionaires in the whole world to take responsibility for sharing their good fortune with their own people—to create hope and sustainability, and to ensure that everyone has the opportunity to take part in the connectivity of our modern world, not just the fortunate few. The principles of Andrew Carnegie could be well learned by others, in understanding the responsibility which comes with good fortune.

2. The Tipping Point

More and more of the rich and the famous are recognising that it is not enough to be personally successful—it's about giving back, to enable everyone to achieve sustenance, security, self-esteem and success—self-determination is everyone's right. When enough people decide to change, we reach a tipping point, when the balance of what is perceived as "the way to be" is tipped over, and big changes happen.

Bill Gates and Warren Buffet are people with enough influence and social capital that they are amongst the most likely people to cause the balance of public opinion to tip. Bill Clinton published his book *Giving* with the same intention to influence people of influence to change their ways. Jimmy and Rosalind Carter founded the Atlanta-based Carter Centre, a non-profit organisation that works to prevent and resolve conflicts, enhance freedom and democracy, and improve health around the world.

It's all too easy to be overwhelmed by the task of "changing the world"—there are so many problems, so many evils and inequities. What you do is just start. Decide to get involved as an Active Citizen and begin. Look around for what needs improved, anything, and put your energy there. It doesn't matter what your particular experience is, there's always something you can do to help. Just make sure you are passionate about whatever it is, and stick with it.

Famous people use their celebrity to highlight causes; professional people use their expertise; rich people use their money—these are forms of energy, and all of us can help in some way. You start with your neighbours, and your local community—your school, church, youth group, care facility—you volunteer, offer your services, give up some of your free time. You just look around and choose something that interests you, and that's where you start.

From monarchy, to billionaires, to film and sports stars, to you—we all can make a difference. Your creativity is part of our world, and by using it, you can have an impact on the future for everyone.

The consumer society is not ultimately satisfying because consuming is not creative—it is passive not pro-active. For people who have everything materially that they need, the absence of meaning and spiritual connection becomes an imperative to be satisfied. Prevailing attitudes of "getting what you want" and "wanting more and more" are not ever going to meet our emotional and spiritual needs—the quest for material security is not the end of the road, it's the beginning.

We are creative creatures, and we need to evolve. More than merely improving our own lives, what we need to do is transform and grow as humans. The paradox of personal development is that, taken to its logical conclusion, it takes us beyond the self, to a deeper purpose that is yours to fulfil—the discovery of meaning over a lifetime, and the understanding of your own potential. How to win friends and influence people takes on an entirely new meaning when you join a project like *Building Wiser Democracies – An Active Citizen Project*. You'll find that you will have fun making a difference.

The behaviour of major corporations has been the subject of much debate for the past few years—greed and exploitation have been amongst the charges levelled at many of the world's major financial institutions and business corporations. If giving back and sharing is to be as important as taking and creating profits for shareholders, companies and corporations need to think carefully about the values which underlie their existence. They need to get involved as well.

The world we live in is one of rapid integration, instant communication and increasing flow of trade, capital, ideas and people. The old models, which ruled our perception of how the world works, need to be reviewed. The prevailing "ideology" of wealth creation is morally and ethically bankrupt, and actual bankruptcy reflects this end-of-the-road energy.

Politicians, famous for jumping on bandwagons and flogging dead horses, are trying to solve our financial crisis by re-inventing wheels on a mode of transport which is outdated when we need a new perspective to define our strategy and our goals.

We are all being affected now by the crumbling edifice of global competition and greed—individual lives, even of the rich and famous, are showing signs of unravelling. We need to find a direction for our energies which is creative and nurturing to all—we need to ask why we're here and what we hope to achieve for everybody. We need to keep our eye on the Big Game, and not get caught up in the power plays.

Bailing out bankers and big industry who have bankrupted the poor and the middle class has a certain legitimacy if it safeguards jobs and savings, but if its end point is merely to allow the very rich to stay very rich, and allow them to continue to take without giving back, then we are using poor people at home and abroad as scapegoats so that the rich can continue in the same way as before.

No lessons have been learned that are morally and ethically useful. Blaming government workers' pensions for the financial situation, and sentencing them to a life of anxiety about their futures is another hypocritical move by those responsible to divert attention from their own role by blaming the victims for their own misfortune.

The opportunity must be grasped to make significant changes—a return to the status quo is not acceptable. In the modern world, our networks of communication include the internet and international financial institutions—the principles of law and order and ethical trust allow these significant communication and cooperation networks to operate efficiently.

Continuing to condone Third World proxy wars as an outlet for unlimited conventional arms sales to rogue states by so-called lawful states is a hypocrisy which needs to be stopped. If the dis-connected states remain as a parallel universe, where the rich nations of the world exploit the commercial opportunities offered by poor countries while paying lip-service to offering aid, we turn a blind eye at our own peril.

Man needs minerals, but minerals can't continue to dominate the life of people to the detriment of the majority and the advantage of the few. The brokers in the commodity markets of the world are some of the best educated people on the planet, but their ethical behaviour is among the worst.

The bill is due paid, and mutual interests must be taken into account. The Age of Exploitation is over, and if the developed world continues to ignore the human rights of the under-developed world, we are committing our own children to a world of constant war, as the oppressed step up their campaign to be heard and included in the abundance of the free world.

We reap what we sow, and we have harvested the mineral abundance of the world without due regard for the rights of peoples for long enough—the tipping point has arrived. Our prosperity as a world community requires that we fully respect the inter-connections between four elements: people, energy, money and social justice.

We all need energy and money in order to survive; we all need to feel secure in order to thrive; we all need to be treated with respect because we are alive. Of all the sins committed by man against man, the worst is to treat others as less than human. The objectification of humans by others is what gives us slavery and exploitation, and leads to holocaust and genocide at the extreme end—it is the root of all evil.

As we have evolved in consciousness, we have come to understand this pivotal idea intellectually, but we don't always follow through into appropriate action. We can stand by and observe human suffering with a detachment born of our us-and-them mentality, a tribal mentality, where we feed our own delusions of superiority by treating others as inferior, and, with a moralistic shaking of the head, stand by while "they" suffer atrocities at the hands of "others", because "they" are not us.
"Treat your neighbour as yourself" is such a powerful injunction because it depends on simple kindness. The Rule of Reciprocity, or the Golden Rule, appears in every society known to man, and it comes down to the same thing—mutual respect for common humanity.

The respect implied by kindness is universally understood; kindness is not in any way condescending or judgemental—it is patient and tolerant, and it understands human frailty. But kindness is strong and gentle at the same time, and kindness can be firm in insisting that the rules of civility are followed. Kindness is not wishy-washy and won't just accept any behaviour. By accepting kindness as our standard, we encapsulate all of the virtues—we exemplify serenity, courage and wisdom. Even the most cynical understand the laws of kindness, and have experienced it, usually from a parent, grandparent or teacher.

The rich and famous have a job to do, just like the rest of us. We all have a duty to create the best world we can for our children and their children—that's the legacy of being human. We can definitely do a better job of it by using our wealth, education and influence in the best way we can think of to make a difference to our world. That's the meaning of success—to use it to influence things for the better.

3. Links between Individuals and Community

We all know people who, by their imagination and determination, make a difference in their local communities, and in the world. Some people make a contribution as individuals and some as members of an organisation or club—the advantage of joining an organization is that your efforts can be multiplies, and you gain the support of a team. Clubs like Round Table, Chamber of Commerce, Lions, Masons, Kiwanis, Legions and Rotary enable individuals to pool their energy to better effect.

We all know people who volunteer, who share their time and their talents, to help others. You may be one of them. By contributing we also gain—as Albert Schweitzer observed:

"There is no higher religion than human service. To work for the common good is the greatest creed."

We all need encouragement, whether to join in or to keep going. By joining together and pooling our resources, we make an even greater difference, and have fun while we are doing it. There are endless opportunities for public private partnerships, in communities and in the world.

Like choosing where to put your energies as an individual, companies and sports organisations can choose something close to their hearts, and pitch in to make a difference. This is not just about donating money—face to face contact is an important element in bringing encouragement and relationship to the equation. The energy and enthusiasm of people meeting people, inspiring effort and perseverance, is the key to lasting success.

Microfinance works because of the connection between people as much as because of the money lent. It brings hope to people and communities where there might be none. It shows people that they are noticed and it encourages them to become self-sufficient and self-determining.

Showing that you care about someone is the most precious gift you can offer—even millionaires like to be noticed. We probably can't, as individuals, make a huge impact on world poverty or war and genocide, but as individuals working together to change the mindset of others who do have the power and the influence to make a difference, we can create a paradigm shift.

Never underestimate the power of the individual. Mahatma Gandhi was one lawyer—by employing *Satyagraha,* non-cooperation or non-violent struggle, and *ahimsa,* an attitude of compassion which transforms suffering and aggression, he changed the world. He won independence for India, inspiring Nelson Mandela and Martin Luther King Jr—the rest, as they say, is history.

4. A Strong Social Conscience

In March 2008, Martin Wolf, chief economics commentator at the Financial Times, announced the death of the dream of global free-market capitalism. In December 2008, Paul Krugman released his book, *The Return of Depression Economics and the Crisis of 2008,* suggesting that Keynesian policy solutions are more relevant than ever. Paul Krugman is a Professor of Economics and International affairs at Princeton University, and an op-ed columnist for the New York Times. His New York Times blog is called *The Conscience of a Liberal.* In 2008, he won the Nobel Prize in Economics for his contributions to New Trade Theory and New Economic Geography. This prize is regarded as the most prestigious prize in the economics field.

My favourite "pioneering economists" are all people with a strong social conscience, and I make no apology for that. Of course there will be some who believe that making money for the rich is the most important role of economists, and no doubt, there are many of them who do. I'll leave you to make your own decision. The word "economics" stems from a Greek word meaning "household management", yet *social-ethical ideals* constantly compete with the *economic anarchy* of a crude, capitalist society, where the idea is to get the most you can, often at the expense of other people—the survival of the fittest. The consequence of this is that the interests of large sections of the population are often not sufficiently protected.

What about human values? Where are they in the vast competitive machinery of intellectual and monetary brilliance? Modern psychological research has conclusively demonstrated that we are motivated by more than just monetary gain. Once we reach a reasonable level of material comfort, more money doesn't necessarily increase our happiness. We all need sustenance and security, and the dignity of work, but we get our greatest satisfaction from making a difference or making a contribution to the greater good—we gain the most self-esteem and pleasure from being able to help others.

The ideas of *wealth creation* and *wealth accumulation* are an extension of the human functions of food production, gathering and storage, which grew into the industrial functions of the production, distribution and consumption of goods and services—the paradigm of *Wealth* is a bi-product of the application of human ingenuity to the resources of the world.

It's about efficiency of scale—as the population grew, we needed to think about more efficient ways to manage resources. We need wealth to nurture life and thrive—we just need to think carefully about what we *all* need from it, and how much of it we each need. We can no longer continue with a model where a very small percentage of the global population holds the majority of the wealth, and the majority of the others are struggling to survive.

5. Using Power Wisely

Christopher Lasch (1932–1994) of New York was a well-known historian, moralist and social critic who worked at the University of Rochester from 1970 until his death in 1994. His book *The Revolt of the Elites and the Betrayal of Democracy* (1996) makes a compelling argument that many of the ills of democracy in the United States arise from the default of elites, their loss of moral values, and their self-serving abandonment of the middle-class and the poor.

Lasch highlights the media and elite educational institutions as a large source of the problem and calls for a return to community and to schools that teach history not self-esteem, and attend to morality, and the teachings of religion. Greatly influenced by Charles Mills, with accurate forecasting he blames those in power for setting in place a system which would further widen the gap between the economic classes, and which has created a crisis in American society.

And what of democracy, the power of the public, composed of discussion circles of peers, where public opinion is the result of each man's deliberation and contribution to the great chorus? If public opinion is not necessarily true, or right or just, who decides? As the rational exertion of political will by individuals is significantly more difficult the larger the society, decisions are increasingly made by small groups of "experts".

Opinion influencing and manipulating becomes an accepted technique of power-holding and power-winning. Spin-doctors and image consultants proliferate, and the modern power elites have increasingly sophisticated means of persuasion. When power is exercised by lobbying, campaign financing, and policy planning networks operating secretly behind closed doors, the public legitimisation of the democratic system is usurped by manipulation. Small circles of people wield huge power.

6. Ethics and Corruption

The question of *ethics* and *corruption* is high in our minds at present, following the global financial crisis, which is perceived as having started in the USA. Why is this? What is there about the culture of the USA which would lead to such wide-scale abuse of the privileges of office? In the corporate era, relations have become impersonal, and the consequence of this is that the executive feels less personal responsibility.

Within the corporate worlds of business and politics, the private conscience is somehow subsumed, and, consequently, ethical standards are institutionalised. If money becomes the one unambiguous criterion of success, the value of things which can't be bought is in danger of being overlooked. If the standards of the moneyed life prevail, the man with money will be respected no matter how he gets it!

Our vocabulary reflects this fundamental change in values, and men can become morally ruthless in the pursuit of easy money—what was once "greed" becomes "good business practice" and "ruthlessness" is admired. When politics and business are too closely linked, public office can be used for private gain.

The network of collusion easily overtakes the proper relationship of business and government—the efficient organisation of society. When complicated expense accounts and bonuses exceed take-home pay, the doors to corruption are wide open. It is "smart" to get away with cheating, and an amoral attitude is celebrated as "business smarts". If success is narrowly related to big money, cynicism and sharp practice will proliferate.

7. Foreign Policy

Foreign policy is the domain of the power elite, and war has become the "business" of some people. In this climate, peace is no longer paramount, and every nation is either friend or foe. When negotiation aimed at peace is seen as "appeasement", and the pride of the nation is linked to "victory", the links between industry and the military require careful scrutiny.

 The economic-military alliance, reinforced since WWII, means that our brightest and best young people are being intensively and explicitly educated to exploit the profit potential inherent in the interdependence of economy and warfare. Big Oil and Big War are two lucrative areas for Big Career.

The military is now the largest single supporter and director of scientific research, and scientific and technological development has shifted from the Space Race (with the downshifting of NASA priorities in the US), to the War Machine and the Atomic Programme.

If the reality of international relations is defined in a military way, whether the mission is called a "peace mission" or not, this emphasises the need for expansion of military facilities, which are then described as "good local employers". The prestige of the military establishment has never been higher, and war is "big business".

We shape ourselves to fit where we want to be—we are creatures of will and creativity. As long as *peace and virtue* are not seen as important, there will be people who are willing to compromise any principle in favour of advancement. The moral distrust of the elite is now so strong as to almost ensure that they are left to their own devices by a public disillusioned by daily reports of corruption in high places.

8. Compassion, Knowledge and Wisdom

An elite network based on *power, wealth and celebrity* is no substitute for an elite network where *compassion, knowledge and wisdom* are prized qualities—neither wealth nor power is necessarily wisdom, and celebrity is only valuable if it rises above the mere existence of fame. Wisdom is based on *ethical conduct* and *character,* both worthy models for imitation and aspiration.

Conduct and character are the result of the thoughtful and intentional application of the values of *Creative Self-Development,* the title of the first book in this series. Policies and practice in a world to be proud of must be based on more than rhetoric and platitude. If vagueness is raised to the position of principle, we are on the rocky road to ruin.

Moral virtue and *meritorious ability* are not old-fashioned, superseded values—they are necessary components for our institutions of governance and learning. Nationally and internationally responsible businesses and political parties must be answerable to voluntary and non-politically affiliated representatives of public opinion.

In today's world, more than ever before, we each have a duty to be part of an appropriate Learning-Circle, to ensure that our voice is heard in the corridors of power. With our educational opportunities never so open, we are able to take our place in the democratic forum of the association or the community, and to contribute to making the world a better place.

The rights to free speech and political participation, which have been hard won, bring with them responsibilities. In a small way, with small steps, it is possible to change the ethical culture of the world. For corruption to continue, it is only necessary for us to continue to sit on the sidelines, to turn a blind eye.

The institutions of our Democracy—education, business and government—started with individuals, who gathered together for the common weal. These institutions may have become machines of power, divorced from our influence, but, if so, this is not irreversible—the cycle turns, and it is time for your voice to be heard—it is time for action. We start with small acts of kindness and consideration. We start by taking part in the community of citizens.

CONCLUSION

Creating a Hopeful Future

Prosperity is the guardian of democracy and peace, but human progress is not all about economic wealth. The *New Democracy Trifecta of People, Relationships and Infrastructure* provides a framework which helps us to focus our efforts on supporting people, supporting fair socio-economic relationships and supporting strong infrastructures and environmental sustainability, and offers us a way to harness our democratic potential on a global scale.

Supporting People – Human Development Potential

In a wise democracy, individuals are important. The individual in a democratic society expects to be respected and creativity and innovation are rewarded. Harnessing human potential means valuing our individual and collective knowledge, training and experience which provide an advantage for global human progress. Providing access to education, healthcare and welfare services maximizes opportunities and potential.

Supporting Relationships – Socio-Economic Potential

Supporting strong socio-economic relationships means providing real opportunities for everyone to contribute to society through meaningful work and fair wages. Public projects are one way of ensuring that every citizen has the dignity of participating in their community and gaining the ability to become an Active and Equal Citizen.

Supporting Infrastructure – Human Survival Potential

Providing and supporting a strong infrastructure is the crucial
dimension of good governance. Enacting policies and procedures
which support processes which allow people to function optimally and
flourish is the specific work of government, and the global dimension
of this work is imperative if our environment and ecology is to be
protected and sustainable for the future.

1. Putting People First

The State, representing the People, has a significant role to play in re-balancing the democratic priorities to put people first, all people, not just the privileged few. Ensuring a dignified life for every citizen is at the centre of the social contract which is Democracy. At present, democracies throughout the world share a dramatic disconnect between public communication and political decision making, where the activity of officials disregards public opinion. We need to somehow rebuild the political infrastructure of Democracy so that public authority can govern in the public interest.

Blaming inept politicians or greedy bankers and corporations ignores the fact that we are all citizens. We can reconfigure our idea of Democracy without apportioning blame if we focus on creating a balance between social, economic and environmental priorities, and on creating a political infrastructure which enables us to address the issues openly. Rethinking the primary rules and values of the political community and its members by engaging everyone in Active Citizenship would address the strain between representative and participative democracy.

2. Accepting the Responsibilities of Citizenship

In a Democracy, citizens are not clients or spectators in politics, although the current response to the global social and economic situation seems to be driven by elite professional politicians and economists. Democracy is predicated on the involvement of citizens in decision making, and democratic politics involves cooperation, consultation, consensus and challenge.

Open Democratic Politics takes place not only in the formal political forum but also in alternative, informal places. Democracy is about choices and careful consideration of competing options, with a view to serving the Common Good, yet reducing the whole of Democratic Politics to a quest for financial stability, performed mostly behind closed doors, reduces the potential for change.

The "unique solution" of austerity has a significantly negative effect on the already disempowered, those who have no resources to weather the storm, while the elites who were responsible for the current crisis go unchallenged and unaffected materially. Conflict is a necessary part of Democracy, embedded in free speech – the right to challenge policies which adversely affect people. Complex and confident political systems accept positive and negative feedback from which they learn by adapting and changing. Wise Democracy is a continuous feedback learning loop, involving public dialogue, civic engagement and compromise.

3. Learning Life's Lessons

By learning the lessons taught by the wise, we create a better world. We do that by living with unpretentiousness and equanimity—we set our minds by the compass of compassion, and endeavour to make a contribution:

"Be the change."
Mahatma Gandhi

The world is full of poor people. Some are poor because they chose to squander their money and their lives on trivia—most are poor because they are exploited and oppressed by rich and powerful people who get richer on the backs of the poor, or who keep what they have in selfish disregard for the suffering of others. We're not financially bankrupted because of the behaviour of poor people—we're morally bankrupted by the behaviour of rich, educated people and their selfish attitude.

"There is no higher religion than human service. To work for the common good is the greatest creed."

Albert Schweitzer

Giving help to those who need it is a necessary part of being human—we give people a helping hand when they are struggling to get by, but charity is a short-term measure. To ensure long-term benefits, we create a society which gives people the opportunity to be self-sustaining through the dignity of work—we ensure that proper reward is given for work, and that work is available. We set up systems so that people are given access to good educational opportunities, good health-care and good housing.

"Education is the most powerful weapon which you can use to change the world."
Nelson Mandela

We give people hope that they can create for themselves a worthwhile future of success, security and significance. That's what we do if we have learned from Life's lessons. The solution is not complicated, and examples are plentiful—we change the world by changing one thing; we change our mindset. By deciding to concentrate on creating a healthy world rather than creating wealth for ourselves, we ensure that we make choices which benefit everyone—we work together to create a life of dignity.

4. Living with Dignity

Creating a life of dignity for all people rests on four pillars:

1. Economic security and sustainability
2. Intellectual freedom and choice
3. Social justice and the rule of law
4. Inclusion in a caring world society

Civil rights are the pivotal axis of a world society where all people are created equal, with equal rights to participation in a world economy. Repression and restriction of these rights by individuals within states is the single most inhuman act at the root of all other evils.

The desire of the privileged elite in any society to prevent its citizens from participating in the abundance of life is the single most destructive challenge to life with dignity for all people.

In world economic terms, Asia is the growth market at the moment, and Africa is next—all continents have a part to play in the creation of the new world of fair opportunity, and no nation can reign supreme over others. The development of a global community is much more than the development of a global market economy, however, though that is a big part of it.

Government concentration on education, healthcare, public welfare, housing, transportation and environmental protection ensures that all people can live a life of dignity. The provision of worthwhile work is a basic pre-requisite for the creation of appropriate self-esteem based on making a contribution to the society in which one lives, within the context of a global society.

Social welfare, social justice and social solidarity are not charity or free gifts—they are the basis of responsible citizenship, and part of our universal social contract. It is the moral and ethical duty of wealthy elites throughout the world to assist others to attain a life of dignity commensurate with an evolved humanitarian society—to do less is to abdicate to the comfort of self-satisfied greed, and an insult to the privilege of success, whether self-created or inherited.

We have the lessons of the wise throughout history to point the way to attain a life of peace, prosperity and joy for all. If we choose to ignore these lessons, we commit the lives of our children and our children's children to an inheritance of fear and want, where the greed of a few fuels the hatred or despair of the many.

5. Reaching the Limit

We have probably almost reached the limit with respect to population growth—the PSR (potential support ratio) is how the United Nations calculates the ratio of people between the ages of fifteen and sixty-four to those above sixty-five. At the moment, America's collective PSR is around five-to-one, meaning there are five people between the ages of fifteen and sixty four for everybody over sixty-five. As our population ages, and births decline, the PSR also decreases—projections indicate that sometime around 2050, humanity will have reached the tipping point, and will begin to depopulate, leveling out at about nine billion.

Birth rates and death rates will even out, but people will live longer, and fewer babies will be born as more of the world urbanizes, and economic development in currently agricultural areas leads to decreasing birth rates. Farming communities traditionally have larger families to work the land and care for the old and the young. Migration is likely to increase, as people seek work in emerging economies, driven by ambition and the motivation to earn a better living. This will tend to increase globalization and level out prosperity—a difficult transition for those in the West, who have enjoyed a higher standard of living by exploiting the resources of the whole world.

Our peaceful co-existence requires that we acknowledge this natural trend—to attempt to hold back the tide of global democratic freedoms is to repress and suppress people's natural tendencies to self-improvement and self-realization. Again, the lessons of history and revolution are there to teach us—the events in the Middle East in February 2011 are testament to this natural trend. The elites of the world would do well to heed these lessons—a peaceful transition to a better distribution of wealth is in all of our best interests. It will happen whether it is supported and welcomed or not.

6. Taking Action - Changing Focus

As long as we allow individual men of influence to manipulate our ideologies, economies, military organizations and politics by their lust for power at any human cost, we will live as we do now. The ideology of *wealth creation* is divisive—supported by a combination of religious and nationalistic fanaticism, military might and economic manipulation, it is ultimately destructive to world peace and detrimental to a hopeful future for the majority of the world's population.

True value lies in people, not money, and the peace and prosperity of the world community rests on healthy connections between four elements: people, natural resources, social justice and money. If we give more weight to money than it deserves, we create a skewed value system, which results in the crisis which we are currently living through—acquisition of wealth and wealth-related status takes precedence over all other behaviour, and greed follows. We all need sustenance and shelter in order to survive, we need to feel secure in order to thrive, and we need to be treated with respect because we are alive.

Cynics will say that such idealism is naïve, that we must be "real" and realize that money is central to life. I want you to question that assumption of our modern culture—the reductionist, materialistic worldview that assumes that money is the measure of all things and that everything must come second to achieving economic growth and the balanced budget. If the tools used for measuring economic growth measure only money, where does that leave the human values of compassion and sustainability. We all need sustenance for the body, security for the mind and significance for the spirit—our souls need love and hope.

We are all in this life together, on planet Earth, and we never stop learning. Our problems do not define who we are, they are just lessons for us to learn from so that we can do things better. We are people of creativity and energy, each able to offer a unique gift to the world—you are valuable just because you are alive and you are able to make a difference. I believe that an affirmation which is culture-neutral, and simple enough for everyone to understand and stand by, can help us to change our focus:

We will create a hopeful future by nurturing people and the environment.

You can make a difference—what do you choose to do?

7. The Importance of International Partnerships

Creating international partnerships offers us all a way to step out of our individual nation state and its particular concerns and focus on ways of re-imagining Democracy without the constriction of a purely economic lens, which serves to perpetuate global competition between nations. Involvement in the international capitalist free-trade system has increased prosperity for some, but the balance needs to be reconfigured to enable more people to enjoy the fruits of that success. Poverty and frustration can only result in more civil unrest.

By working in partnership, across borders and boundaries, we can change the policies and institutions which make the rich richer and the poor poorer at home and abroad. We can advocate for policies and support initiatives that respect the integrity of every human being, and offer the dignity of social inclusion to everyone, by supporting children, families and communities as they develop the capacities to solve their own problems.

8. A Compassionate Community Starts with You

A compassionate society starts with *you*. You are important, and you have a contribution to make to improve our world. You change the world by caring for your neighbours and your community. Gradually, the circle of your community will extend out as a *loving circle* which can embrace the whole world. You are never alone in this enterprise—help will appear from the most amazing places. By having the intention, and following through on it in our reality, we create an *energy magnet* which pulls in other sources of positive energy:

Today, *200 million* people worldwide are still thought to be living and working in conditions of near slavery. In the developing world, more than *1.2 billion* people live below the international poverty line, earning less than $1.25 per day. Among this group of poor people, many have problems obtaining adequate, nutritious food for themselves and their families. As a result, *815 million* people in the developing world are undernourished. They consume less than the minimum amount of calories essential for sound health and growth. [www.freedomfromhunger.org/info]

So freedom and equality for all men, women and children, regardless of colour and creed, is an ongoing challenge, and our challenge today, as a world community, is still to extend these rights to every person. Our individual challenge is to examine ourselves with respect to our own individual needs and desires, and to combine them with the needs of *collective social justice*. This is not easy, yet with passion and perseverance, we continue to take one step at a time towards the goal of world peace, love and joy. We achieve our intentions by keeping them foremost in our mind, and we do that by ensuring that we keep things *simple*, and make them as *enjoyable* and *practical* as possible.

We start with the young and we ensure that they are aware of the *true history* of the search for freedom and equality for all people, and the *true value* of this ideal. We learn best by doing, so we encourage compassion and cooperation from an early age, and we lead by example.

We encourage community involvement, and we enable people to experience the joy of creative participation in the community, with the intention to make a difference. When we truly feel part of our environment, we find pleasure in improving it, and we take justifiable pride in individual and collective accomplishments.

Living creatively starts with knowing your Life is important and that you can help to change the world. Don't delay - start today.

We are the government and the government is us. Our collective actions can change our world.

THE CREATIVE LEARNING SERIES

The *Creative Learning Series* is designed to help you to develop your talents and explore your potential, improve your awareness and enhance your quality of life. By being creative, you develop the skills of enterprise, imagination, curiosity, risk taking and courage, which enhance your capabilities and capacities. You develop an enthusiasm and a joie de vivre which will bring joy to you and which will be inspiring to other people. Creativity is about growing and evolving, looking into things with an enquiring and open mind, and living a life of purpose and passion.

Here you will find plans, tools and techniques to support your personal development or that of your company, corporation or organization, and to increase our shared potential to make a difference in the wider community. In the modern world, it is increasingly necessary for each of us to have a way of looking at the big picture, and participating in the solutions to the world's problems, using our talents and our creativity to make a real difference.

The fourteen books and projects of *The Creative Learning Series* aim to inspire people everywhere to create a kinder world. You can learn to create your best life and our best world at the same time through *Creative Lifelong Learning* and *Creative Action Planning*. This social enterprise and collaborative initiative invites you to work together in partnership, using your particular skills and knowledge, to make things better for everyone. Each book in the series examines a different aspect of personal, social, professional and spiritual development, and invites you to participate by harnessing your *Creative Imagination*.

Creative Lifelong Learning is about fulfilling your own potential and also about working together to support things like advancing democracy, extending educational and employment opportunities, improving health, and alleviating poverty. It facilitates the exchange of experience and support through fellowship and partnership, as wise relationships are crucial in expanding the true understanding that we are all the same in our humanity.

Creative Action Planning harnesses the power of human imagination or consciousness to create meaningful and sustainable development - we generate an idea, we organize the elements which will enable us to proceed and then we develop the plan through direct action. Individuals transform the world by working together in partnership, and *"It does not have to be this way"* is the thought which drives the progress of human civilization.

We each have a gift to enable us to contribute, and we are equally responsible for the outcome. We all have different ways of doing things, and we all have gifts which bring satisfaction to us, and which can be used to help others. By being the best you can be, you help others to be the best they can be. By bringing your talents to the team and working together to improve things for everyone, you are able to make the best use of your talents, and make a contribution to the development of our shared Human Potential.

You are invited to join this global project and to encourage partners to work together with purpose and passion to make a difference in our world.

Book One – Creative Self-Development – Discover and Share Peace of Mind, Love of Life and Joy.
(Special Abridged Edition – Creative Self-Development – Creating the Unique Tapestry of Your Life)
Learn the art of creative self-development. Free your imagination and realize your full potential. Find out how your mind works, and how you can develop your consciousness over time to be all you can be.

Book Two – Life's Lessons – Working Together to Transform Education, Business and Government.
(Special Abridged Edition – Life's Lessons – Evolving Strong Democracy by Sharing Success)
Explore the development of Democracy throughout the world from 1776 to the present day, and consider how we can advance Democracy by sharing success and by transforming the key organizations of Education, Business and Government. By refocusing on our shared values and creating more inclusive societies, we can create a future worth living for our children and our children's children.

Book Three – Gifts from Yggdrasil – A Hero Quest for Today.
This interactive novel is your invitation to join the Hero Quest which is as old as humankind, and which is described in different ways by every culture, but always has the same aim – to create the best world we can imagine. If you are interested in venturing forth as a hero to find the answers to the problems of our world, this quest might be for you.

Book Four – Stress-Free Lifelong Learning – A Guide to Effective and Enjoyable Education for Everyone.
This International Project is designed for all Lifelong Learners, and whether you are a student, parent, educator leader or politician, this guide is designed for you. It offers strategies to enhance learning and teaching, and to encourage, inspire and connect individuals and organizations who want to help promote stress-free Lifelong Learning.

Book Five – Spirit's Gifts and Soul's Mission – A Course in Wise Relationships

By engaging in Wise Relationships, we can all transform our societies and our religions. This International Project invites you to become a partner and to join together with others to plan how we can bring reconciliation and peace to the religious strife which threatens the security and wellbeing of so many people throughout the world.

Book Six – At Peace with the World – A Little Book of Encouragement for Everyday Heroes

The twenty short stories in this book highlight everyday heroes who help ordinary people in their own communities by freely sharing their skills. These stories are designed to raise a smile, and raise your spirits. This book is for potential heroes and those everyday heroes who are already playing a part in making the world a better place, one person at a time.

Book Seven – Planning for Success – Going for the Win-Win in the Game of Life

By joining this International Project, you can explore all aspects of the successful life, and also work together with other people to maximise success for your community, organization or country. Planning is a process of choosing among the many options, and it is a skill which can be learned by practice. If you are failing to plan appropriately, you are wasting your energy and your time. Taking the time to undertake this project may be time well spent…

Book Eight – Building Wiser Democracies – An International Active Citizenship Project.

This International Active Citizenship Project invites you to find partners to change the Democracy Script from the exclusively economic, to a more human-scaled and accessible script of personal, socio-economic and environmental wellbeing. Just as the democratic movements of the eighteenth century focused on three ideals, Freedom, Equality and Justice, we can rethink democracy for the twenty-first century by focusing on a New Democracy Trifecta– People, Relationships and Infrastructure.

Book Nine – Harnessing the Pioneer Spirit - An Exploration of Possibilities and Potentials

This exploration of the Pioneer Spirit looks at all kinds of pioneers, past and present, and invites you to think about your own potential to explore new horizons. I hope you gain inspiration from this exploration of the Pioneer Spirit, just as I did.

Book Ten – Creating Our Best World – A Global Mindfulness Project

Mindfulness provides a win-win where you can find peace of mind and success for yourself and also help create a better world by working with partners on the project of your choice. The ABC of Mindfulness offers you a simple way to include Mindfulness in your daily life and the Mindfulness Script provides a method to work with partners worldwide to engage in positive change. Come and join us. You can make a difference.

Book Eleven - Choosing More Mindful Pathways - Living a Life of Purpose and Passion

This book is the sequel to *Creating Our Best Life – A Global Mindfulness Project*. It is designed to enable you to explore more ways you can include Mindfulness in your life and enjoy the advantages at home, at work and in the world. The decision to choose more mindful pathways is the first step on your journey to success.

Book Twelve - Building Pathways to Peace - Some Lessons in Mindfulness for World Leaders

The successful participants in this course will gain an increased potential to release new creative energy back into the world by solving the problems which are blocking our progress towards peace. Wherever conflict continues in the world, people suffer and poverty and pain proliferate. Mindful leadership is needed to move things on, and building pathways to peace is a way to begin the process of change.

Book Thirteen – The Creative Lifelong Learning Formula – Building Global Partnerships for a Sustainable World

The Creative Lifelong Learning Formula includes the key elements of *Creative Lifelong Learning* from the twelve books of *The Creative Learning Series*, as well as the tools and techniques for *Creative Action Planning*, which are currently only available as individual E-Learning projects.

Here, you will discover how you can design your own Lifelong Learning pathway, create action plans to realize your potential, and become a partner in the *UN Global Strategy*. *The Creative Lifelong Learning Formula* offers a range of creative strategies and action plans to move the process along, and the *UN Global Goals* offer a comprehensive blueprint to focus your energies to help create a better world for all of us.

Book Fourteen – God and the Global Kindness Business – An Evolving Story of Partnership, Progress and Human Potential

What could be more important than creating a world of peace and plenty for all? *The Global Kindness Business* provides a way to join together with other partners and achieve the ultimate goal of world peace. This is a guide for partners who want to actively do the work of creating a kinder world, one step at a time.

In 100 steps, you can become inspired, informed and involved in *The Global Kindness Business* which has been helping people make progress since the beginning of time. Choose your pathway and your companions, and set out to change your life and our world. You won't regret it.

To become a partner in *The Global Kindness Business*, all you need to do is set out to try your best to make a difference. You can choose to make a difference locally, nationally or internationally, and wherever you start, your efforts will resonate throughout the interconnected system which is our shared world. The voices of individual people raised together are needed to encourage world leaders to work together and to help us create a more hopeful future for everyone.

My Personal Perspective on Progress and Success

Success is attained by the steady achievement of meaningful goals, and for me the goals are as follows:

1. Working together with global partners to create a kinder, fairer, world.
2. Supporting stress-free lifelong learning.
3. Advancing democracy by sharing success.
4. Aiming for peace and plenty for everyone.
5. Leaving the world a better place.

Expressed as a *Creative Action Plan* it looks like this:

My intention is to work with others to create a kinder, fairer world, and to leave the world a better place. I will succeed in this by:

1. Promoting effective and enjoyable *Creative Lifelong Learning* for everyone by sharing what I have learned in over forty years of helping people of all ages to progress successfully towards their goals.
2. Developing the *Creative Action Planning Process* and inviting people to form partnerships to create a kinder, fairer and more sustainable world.
3. Writing the *Creative Learning Series* to encourage people throughout the world to think carefully about how they can help to make the world a better place.

I hope that you find some inspiration and ideas in the *Creative Learning Series*. If you have, I have succeeded. If you help one person to live a better life, you help the whole world. Every good deed is potentially gifted forward, and the Creative Energy in the world is increased. I wish you every success in your life going forward, and encourage you to share your gifts freely.

About the Author

Ann Miller is a Scottish-Canadian Creative Lifelong Learning Specialist, author of *The Creative Learning Series*.

https://www.amazon.com/author/creativelearningseries

www.ingramcontent.com/pod-product-compliance
Lightning Source LLC
Chambersburg PA
CBHW031310250726
48656CB00005B/1725